WHAT MEN ARE SAYING ABOUT
I AM MAN ENOUGH

Asa Leveaux's *I Am Man Enough* dispels society's myths of what it means to be a man and provides self-empowering affirmations for standing in the full monty of "Yes" to confidently, virtuously, and creatively express one's masculine gifts. Know that the book you hold in your hands is a tool of healing and transformation. Please take advantage of it.
- **Michael Bernard Beckwith**
Author of *Life Visioning*

I was SPRINKLED and connected to the possibility of manhood!
- **Jonathan Sprinkles**
Best Selling Author of *Presentation Power*

Author and Entrepreneur, Asa Leveaux has written a brilliant how to guide called *I Am Man Enough: 365 Affirmations For Men*. As a fashion designer who designs for savvy men who are global thinkers, I recommend his current publication as a must read for all men of style. Since personal style initially emanates from within, I strongly feel this book

fortifies a man's resolve to constantly aspire to find his better self. It's a fascinating read that not only encourages men to become more self-aware, seek self-improvement, but also continually empower one another! It's an awesome well-written publication from an engaging and fabulous author!
- **Sabre Mochachino**
Founder and Creative Director
of Mochachino: Los Angeles | New York

Our society measures men almost solely by the state of their career and money. Yet a career and money comes from self-knowledge and all the 'soft stuff' Asa gets into here. Asa's book can help you get to know yourself, to try new ideas and challenges, which lead to the failures and successes that build the confidence needed to lead to greater and greater things, anywhere in money, family or life.
-**Aaron Ross**
Bestselling Author of *Predictable Revenue*

*I love the idea of **I Am Man Enough** AND its execution. As someone who published my own book with a "365 days of inspiration" concept (My Gratitude Journal), I know a thing or two about daily affirmations. When we build ourselves up, it automatically prevents us from putting ourselves down. This book makes me smile and gives me a warm feeling in my heart. I'm a man and hear me roar! Asa Leveaux is not only brilliant, but also has* an incredible, one-of-a-kind personality that draws people in like bees to honey. He's a true visionary and we're lucky he has affirmed himself and is sharing his mission with the world.

-Russ Terry
Founder/CEO, Life Coach Radio Networks

I Am Man Enough is a must read! From the affirmations mentioned in this book to the inspiring words of the author, I couldn't put the book down. Everyone has so much going on in his or her lives and we're all trying to stay healthy with our workouts and diets. But daily personal affirmations are equally important. Currently being in a new business venture, this book is just what I need to keep me on track and focused on the bigger picture. Thank you Asa!

- Timothy J. Bance
Founder & CEO of The Ego Studio
(Casting & Development)

I Am Man Enough: 365 Affirmations for Men, is the bold new work by Asa Leveaux. His use of affirmations provide needed healing and help to reshape not only the perception of manhood, but its very definition which makes this a must read for every man both young and old.

- Aaron L. Ashford
Licensed Therapist and Author

I AM MAN ENOUGH

---

365 AFFIRMATIONS FOR MEN

ASA LEVEAUX

Published by Phoenix Ink Publishing

A Leveaux Group Company

First published by Phoenix Ink Publishing, 2015

Copyright © 2015 by Asa Leveaux.
All rights reserved

No part of this book may be reproduced in any form without written permission in advance from the publisher.

Inquiries regarding permission for use of the material contained in this book should be addressed. Thank you for supporting writers and creativity.

Printed in the United States of America
ISBN: 978-0-9885002-6-6

OTHER BOOKS BY ASA LEVEAUX

365 Erotic Reasons Why I Love You
Why I Won't Hire Black People

DEDICATION

To the little boy in all of us

CONTENTS

Introduction 11
Personal Affirmation Story— Vic Carter 16
Personal Affirmation Story— Emmanuel Dagher 19
Personal Affirmation Story— Josh George 23
Personal Affirmation Story— Denny Morales 26
Personal Affirmation Story— Dr. Wayne Pernell . 28
Personal Affirmation Story— Marcus Brown 30
Personal Affirmation Story— Brett Zachman 32
365 Daily Affirmations For Men 35

INTRODUCTION

It was February 5, 2014 at 1:55 am and I was trying to find a reason why being a man was a good thing; I wanted to share the great news with my son. I thought to myself, "It shouldn't be this difficult to explain to someone you love the best trait that you share." However, in that moment it was. I, like you, now live in the digital age and I wanted to know if other men could assist me, so I went somewhere to get assistance—social media. I posed the question to my friends and followers knowing that there would be at least one person who would remind me of a greatness I bring to the world as the result of being a man. Unexpectedly, I found nothing.

As I am writing this, men around the world are watching video clips and reading magazine articles, and they are in discussions where women are being reminded of their power, beauty and value. I am grateful that women receive affirmations through various mediums and platforms because it is important. As a man I must ask the following: Do we not deserve to be affirmed? Do we not deserve to be publicly valued? Is man merely a being that has a penis and is responsible for all of the ills of the world?

There was a time when I felt that I was a person with a penis with multiple problems. As someone who has been a leader in combat, I know what it's like to care and provide for those that follow you and then to wrestle with the loneliness of leadership. As a proud father of a little boy, I know the joy of assisting in the creation of life and the empty taste of realizing that you don't know the first thing about being someone's daddy because you are a fatherless father. I know the chronic sting of losing someone that you loved with the very lining of your heart and having the need to infect an undeserving soul with the pain you possess.

You, like me, are not the totality of your past limitations. I had to learn that there is more to me than what I see.

I believe in the possibility of manhood. I first learned about the possibility of what a man could be when I was in kindergarten. At the age of five I saw a peacock up close and personal in my class. I marveled at the feathers and how they were saturated in colors. Internally I thought the walk of a peacock resembled the walk of the men in my family and at church. I liked that walk. I fell in love with a bird that day. As if my admiration could not be any more sincere, I learned that only male peacocks were "beautiful." I thought to myself, "WHAT? You mean that men can be beautiful?" Now, at 31 years of age, I see many men who do not consider themselves the way that I saw that bird. This is true because others do not affirm men, in my experience, or, most important, they are not affirmed by themselves.

What are affirmations? Affirmations are positive declarations and statements. Affirmations are used to transform your ideas about yourself. Affirmations are expressed in the present tense and focus on what you want rather than what you don't want on a consistent basis. Affirmations are tools to change the looped recordings of years of limited thinking and beliefs that no longer serve you.

My intention for you is that you read an affirmation each day. I know that you are capable of consuming this book within a few days. I hope reading this book is not something to check off your list, but rather I hope that reading it causes a continuous transformational process in your mind. To ensure that you understand the gravity of the process that will begin in the coming pages, I have asked a few men to share their stories of how affirmations have changed the trajectories of their lives. I believe that you will gain information about how to implement these life-enriching affirmations in your life.

I want you to live a life that is saturated in self-actualized genius! I desire that you not only speak positivity into your life but you also conceive thoughts on how to make that thought a living and breathing result. For example, after every affirmation that you encounter there will be a "Genius Thought". The purpose behind the "Genius Thought" is that you begin to mentally construct the course of action to cause real change. An instance of this would be if you said the affirmation, "I am a reflection of masculine love", your mind may immediately say, "Are you crazy? NO YOU ARE NOT!" which would not feel good. However, if you added the "Genius Thought" with, "How am I a reflection of masculine love?" then that would begin the process of becoming the man you wish to be.

Action is the cure for what ails you. This statement is not merely theory but rather experience. If you are depressed, take action. If you are scared, take action. If you are hopeless, take action. If you are hungry, take action. If you are lonely, take action. If you are temporarily without funds, take action. I believe in action so much that I desire for you to begin to take action in your life. For each affirmation you will experience a moment set aside for you to write down what action step you will take in an effort to make the affirmation real for you. I look forward to hearing from you as to what action you decide for yourself.

As a result of reading this book, you (or the man in your life) will understand the power, divinity, fortitude and mastery that you possess by being the man you are **now**. I emphasize the word "now" because you are enough where you currently reside. The fact that you are ENOUGH does not depend on your race, culture, bank account, possessions, number of sexual partners or lack thereof, sexuality, penis size, education level, family structure, past hurts, current addiction or feelings of inadequacy. YOU ARE MAN ENOUGH!

Asa Leveaux
Chief Genius Activator
Founder of Genius Academy™

PERSONAL AFFIRMATION STORY— VIC CARTER

I have always believed in the power of words; how they are arranged, how they are chosen, but, most important, how and when they are delivered. Properly placed prose can enlighten, entertain and stir emotion. Words can also motivate and provide an insight that becomes engrained for a lifetime of multiple uses.

The words of two men have greatly affected my life, and they are words that were delivered, as they say in the church, right on time! The first came in a casual conversation over lunch with Colin Powell, four-star general, at the New York Hilton in August 1989. I asked him if he ever experienced racism as a general in the United States Army. His response was, "Yes, I have. But here's the thing: Racism is not my problem. It's theirs." Wow—short yet powerful.

Another man whose booming voice was heard around the world offered another tidbit of advice that has always driven me. Mal Goode was the first African American network news correspondent; he claimed the job with ABC News in September 1962. "I wasn't sure if I was going to take that job, so I called my good friend, Jackie Robinson who told me I'd be a fool not to take it." During that conversation Jackie gave Mal a piece of advice—, which he in turn gave to me. He said: "No matter what you do, don't let anyone break your will!"

"Racism is not my problem. It's theirs." and "Don't let them break your will!" I am a black boy from Radford, Virginia. I grew up in a modest three-bedroom home with my hard-working parents and four sisters. I have seen and experienced racism and I have had "them" (which is sometimes "us") try to break my will, keep me from my dreams, hold me back, tell me it can't be done, make fun of me because I "talked like a white boy"—but I did not listen. I did not relent. I did not hold back. I stayed focused on my goals. I graduated from college on a Friday and appeared on television as a reporter on Monday—and here I remain today. For the past 20 years, I have occupied the anchor chair at the highly rated CBS station. I have interviewed or met seven presidents of the United States and reported on stories from four continents and 15 countries. I was blessed to do this because of a relentless faith in God--a belief that it can be done--and casting a deaf ear to those who would try to break my will. Control your **_will_** and control your **_destiny_**.

- Vic Carter is the principal evening anchor at CBS WJZ-TV in Baltimore, MD.

PERSONAL AFFIRMATION STORY— EMMANUEL DAGHER

Athletes who are dedicated to keeping the condition of their bodies at an optimum state through exercise know that in order to do so, they need a specific formula. This formula usually consists of some, if not all, of the following things:

1. A willingness to maintain an optimum physical state.
2. Consistency and repetition with following through on their desired physical state.
3. Finding the joy in keeping themselves fit, so that when the immediate passion fizzles they are still fueled into creating the palpable end-result they seek.

Just as the body thrives on physical exercise with the implementation of the three steps shared in the above formula, positive affirmations with the combination of the three steps listed above have the power to do the same for the mind.

Affirmations have greatly helped me create more ease and fulfillment in every area of my life. However, the kinds of affirmations I work with are not focused on the specifics of a desired outcome; they are focused on the qualities that are at the root of the specific desired outcome.

For example: One could say, "I want to manifest winning a 10 million dollar lottery." Although this method of being specific may work for some people, a limited number of people will see a lasting result. What I usually do is ask myself a question like, "What qualities will winning 10 million dollars bring into my life?" I usually receive an answer such as: it provides me with a sense of freedom, flow, ease, peace, trust, faith, grace, and so on.

When I refine my affirmation to something like, "I choose to create greater freedom and flow in my life, especially with my finances," I actually open myself up to experiences and opportunities that I may not have been available to before had I remained fixed on winning that 10 million dollar lottery ticket. I also save myself from a great deal of disappointment when I expand from specifics and into the qualities I'm seeking to experience.

To take it a step further with my affirmations, I have daily check-ins with myself to see where I am already seeing qualities in my life that I intend to expand. The Universe knows no "size." What may seem small to one person may be huge for someone else. When I started to realize I already have some of the desired qualities I'd like more of, I started to notice that I was no longer attached to *how* things showed up, and was more interested in my quality of life. It's like a miracle to the rational mind when we are able to let go of the attachments we create around manifesting certain desired outcomes, and living in the flow of life. In fact, living in the flow is where we are at our most open and available to create some of the greatest blessings in our lives.

The final thing I'd like to share is that I always open up every affirmation from a space of knowing that what I desire is already done. So rather than using phrases like "I want" or "I hope," which are not really coming from a powerful knowing that it's already done, I use phrases like "I now choose . . ." or "I am creating . . ." or "I now step into . . ."

With just these few little refinements, I have witnessed extraordinary results in my life and in my client's lives when it comes to using affirmations. I know, that if implemented, they will also support you too.

Love,
Emmanuel Dagher

Emmanuel is a spiritual teacher, author, speaker, and kindred friend who enjoys co-creating great joy and miracles with others.

PERSONAL AFFIRMATION STORY— JOSH GEORGE

A person is never defined by any one thing they do. It sounds like an obvious statement, but it is something that I found very difficult to learn. I am an athlete. I have been one my whole life, and I am a relatively good one. Every day I train for up to six hours as a long distance track racer and marathoner. This is a schedule I have repeated six days a week, for the past twelve years, constantly striving to eek out every last drop of potential my body has to offer. With that much time dedicated to a single goal, it was far too easy for me to wrap up my self-worth entirely in my athletic performance and, despite my best efforts, performances were not always at the level I wanted them to be.

It is inadvisable for anyone to tie up their self-worth in a singular aspect of their life, and this is especially true for athletes. When you win, you feel like you can leave with the ten at the bar and solve world hunger on the drive home, and when you lose you feel like you are a failure at life.

Having your self-worth tied solely to your athletic accomplishments does not seem so bad when you are winning. Victory breeds happiness, which breeds confidence, which breeds success. As long as you keep winning, you are fine. Rare is the individual who knows nothing but victory. And therein lies the problem.

In a highly successful career in which I have competed and medaled in three Paralympics and two world championships (and counting), I have also endured extended periods of time where I could not win a race if the fate of the world depended on it. After a quick rush to the top of the international rankings, it was quite a shock to the system when I found myself entangled in a web of poor performances. Losing was never in the forecast and when it started happening, I did not know how to handle it. Losses would create self-doubt that would creep outside of my racing world and infect every other aspect of my life: relationships, friendships, and professional motivation. Previous losses would affect future races. At the start of one race I would still be thinking about the finish of the last. More importantly, I began questioning who I was as a person more and more with each consecutive loss. In my delusional line of thinking, each poor performance was a direct representation of who I was as a person.

For nearly three years I lost the battle with losing, until a wise and wonderful friend helped me realize that I had the equation completely backwards. How I perform in a race does not dictate who I am as a person, but rather, who I am as a person dictates how I race. At the beginning of each race I began mumbling to myself my new affirmation: Who I am now is who I will be at the finish whether I win or lose.

One race does not a person make, for we are all more than any one thing. Whether I win or lose, at the end of the day I am still a son, brother, boyfriend, best friend, good, kind, funny, thoughtful, inquisitive, happy, goofy, corny, *successful*—not just an athlete. While it may be the icing on the cake when you can be all those things and have a gold medal around your neck, I know that at bare minimum I'll still be eating cake at the end of the day.

- Joshua George is a Paralympic Gold Medalist and record holder, marathon enthusiasts and motivational speaker

PERSONAL AFFIRMATION STORY— DENNY MORALES

Knowing that we are creatures of habit, we tend to get lost in our thoughts. I remember waking up one day when a buddy handed me Robert Kiyosaki's book, *Rich Dad Poor Dad*. I hated to read, so I pushed myself a little bit, but that's all it took. I couldn't take my eyes off of those pages. This woke me up to a world I never realized I was already in. I couldn't stop reading. I was killing like ten books a month. The local bookstore was my home. I pretty much camped out reading every spiritual, self help, and business book I could get my hands on.

That was my foundation to begin the journey of telling myself a different story through daily affirmations. When I did this my world turned into the good kind of chaos. Everything that needed to leave my life left. I opened up new space to allow new love in my life. This led me to create a film with people like: Jack Canfield, Tony Hsieh, John Gray, etc. I just finished my first book, and am working on several feature films and TV shows. Things just flow to me now. No more chasing; it actually chases me. Now, I'm learning how to say no to all the amazing offers that come into my life so I can maintain my energy. Not that I don't love the projects, but we must maintain focus. Now, I remind others of who they are. They call me the Allspark.

-Denny Morales is an Emmy Award winner and Executive Producer at Watery Flame Productions where their mission is to provide mainstream inspirational, transformational entertainment for the light-hearted, optimistic and progressive viewer.

PERSONAL AFFIRMATION STORY— DR. WAYNE PERNELL

Beginning a phrase with the words "I Am" initiates power in your life. For so long, so many of us have told ourselves things like, "I'm . . . not ready . . . not good enough . . . not fit enough . . . not wealthy enough." We hurt ourselves by invoking the power of "I Am" and we come to a conclusion that we just might not be *enough*.

But that begs a new question, if we think it through and this, then, reflects my journey: "Enough for whom?"

When that question surfaced, my life changed.

"I AM" preceded more powerful, healthy, and focused words. I began to measure myself against words that became a personal vision for how I wanted to live in the world.

   I am dynamic.
    I am loving.
     I am engaged.

I took on the day knowing that's who I was becoming in every moment. I lay down to rest at the end of the day assessing how I had lived up to my ideal. By being more alive and dynamic, my life became (and continues to become) more joyful. By bringing more joy out of myself, I began serving others more deeply. As I engage in the world from a loving place, compassion rules my judgments. Staying compassionate and curious puts me in a place to appreciate others, for who they are, not who I want them to be.

Affirmations are the rocket fuel of intentions. Where are you headed? Aim high! Light the fuse and live into your bigger, better self!

- Dr. Wayne Pernell is dedicated to guiding the discovery of emerging strengths, personal power, and magic in people's daily lives. He is the author of "Choosing Your Power: Becoming Who You Deserve to be, at Home and in the World!"

PERSONAL AFFIRMATION STORY— MARCUS BROWN

I came to an understanding of affirmations by the use of The Law of Attraction. I was in a bad car wreck in 2008, which left me paralyzed from the waist down. Also in the wreck, I lost a loved one. I was down and depressed for weeks, until I took it upon myself to switch my focus. I knew that if I wanted to progress and get myself back to where I was, I could no longer be in a of *why me* frame of mind and feel sorry for myself. I had to man up. Being down, didn't mean I was out.

So, while lying there in the hospital bed I began to tell myself: I will walk again. I will finish college and I will be successful. At the time I didn't even know that what I was doing was using affirmations. Some months passed and I slowly started regaining feeling in my legs. A friend had told me about this book/movie *The Secret* and how powerful it is. The secret is The Law of Attraction, which is energy attracts like energy. I came to find out that everything is made up of energy, even thoughts and words. This understanding gives way to affirmations, because everything you think, say, or do you are attracting back to you. The key is to use it in the present tense, as if you already have it, and to truly believe that you will attract what you really want.

Once I fully understood this concept I put all of my focus and energy into it to progress even further. I was now saying my body is fully healed; I'm in college with a degree on the way and I'm successful in whatever I do. Now that it is 2015, I am proud to say I got my college degree, I have a successful job and I run my own business, and I can walk with arm crutches. I'm even more proud to say that I am slowly progressing to a cane. I'm still not fully where I want to be, but I am surely not where I used to be.

Before I go, I'm going to leave you with this question. Are you man enough to take control of your life?

- Marcus Brown is an Image Coordinator and Graphic Artist residing in Oklahoma City, OK

PERSONAL AFFIRMATION STORY— BRETT ZACHMAN

My name is Brett Zachman. I go by my nickname "Zach." I'm not writing today about nicknames, but about the power of words. Specifically, how I believe "thoughts" are "things." In my life, affirmations have spoken fantasies into realities.

On January 1, 2014, I turned 43 and set a goal to run 1 mile every morning for 43 mornings. As an ex-athlete, I use positive habits in the area of physical fitness to push myself. This goal was an exercise in discipline. Discipline creates patterns, patterns become habits, and habits shape your life.

During my morning runs, I have a series of 10 affirmations spoken 10 times each in a specific order:

"I am perfectly comfortable emotionally, mentally, and physically speaking in front of large crowds!"

"I am comfortable setting healthy boundaries with women, and I do!"

"I am comfortable living alone and choosing to focus on self!"

"To meet my physical needs, I will seek the hands of a loving woman!"

"I am Zach; I am clean! I am Zach; I am innocent! I am Zach; I am pure!"

"I am Zachariah; I live in remembrance of God!"

"I am Zachariah; I'm a memory of God!"

"As a man amongst men, I am the great encourager!"

"I am a son of God, a brother in Christ and fierce spirit warrior!"

"I bring the gifts of love, hope, and encouragement. My purpose is to build character and integrity with humility. I envision a world of passion and playfulness in service to God!"

In 2014, I was promoted to a senior vice president in our company. Relationships with myself, sons, family, and team are extraordinary. In addition, I attracted a wonderful woman who is capable of becoming my first true-life partner. Apparently, words do matter!

Brett "Zach" Zachman is the founder of BeMen, which can be found at www.bemen.org

365 DAILY AFFIRMATIONS FOR MEN

1. I am more than my penis.

GENIUS THOUGHT: How am I more than my penis?

_____
_____
_____
_____
_____
_____
_____

GENIUS ACTION: What action step is required of me to make this affirmation a maximized reality?

_____
_____
_____
_____
_____
_____
_____

2. The divine made me the way I was meant to be.

GENIUS THOUGHT: Why did the divine make me?

_____
_____
_____
_____
_____
_____

GENIUS ACTION: What action step is required of me to make this affirmation a maximized reality?

_____
_____
_____
_____
_____
_____

3. My ancestors created me in love.

GENIUS THOUGHT: Why did my ancestors create me in love?

_____
_____
_____
_____
_____
_____
_____

GENIUS ACTION: What action step is required of me to make this affirmation a maximized reality?

_____
_____
_____
_____
_____
_____
_____

4. I am more than a commodity.

GENIUS THOUGHT: Why am I more than a commodity?

___

GENIUS ACTION: What action step is required of me to make this affirmation a maximized reality?

___

5. The essence of me is limitless.

GENIUS THOUGHT: Why is my essence limitless?

_____
_____
_____
_____
_____
_____
_____

GENIUS ACTION: What action step is required of me to make this affirmation a maximized reality?

_____
_____
_____
_____
_____
_____
_____

6. I have the capability to love with the force of seven supernovas.

GENIUS THOUGHT: Why do I have the capability to love with the force of seven supernovas?

_____
_____
_____
_____
_____
_____
_____

GENIUS ACTION: What action step is required of me to make this affirmation a maximized reality?

_____
_____
_____
_____
_____
_____
_____

7. I am the strength in my daughter's fairy tales.

GENIUS THOUGHT: Why am I the strength in my daughter's fairy tales?

_____
_____
_____
_____
_____
_____
_____

GENIUS ACTION: What action step is required of me to make this affirmation a maximized reality?

_____
_____
_____
_____
_____
_____
_____

8. My son is the jewel of society.

GENIUS THOUGHT: Why is my son the jewel of society?

_____
_____
_____
_____
_____
_____
_____

GENIUS ACTION: What action step is required of me to make this affirmation a maximized reality?

_____
_____
_____
_____
_____
_____
_____

9. The sun bows when I smile.

GENIUS THOUGHT: Why does the sun bow when I smile?

_____
_____
_____
_____
_____
_____
_____

GENIUS ACTION: What action step is required of me to make this affirmation a maximized reality?

_____
_____
_____
_____
_____
_____
_____

10. The earth welcomes the skin I'm in.

GENIUS THOUGHT: Why does the earth welcome the skin I'm in?

_____
_____
_____
_____
_____
_____
_____

GENIUS ACTION: What action step is required of me to make this affirmation a maximized reality?

_____
_____
_____
_____
_____
_____
_____

11. I am the freshest thing since fresh fallen citrus.

GENIUS THOUGHT: Why am I so fresh?

_____
_____
_____
_____
_____
_____

GENIUS ACTION: What action step is required of me to make this affirmation a maximized reality?

_____
_____
_____
_____
_____
_____

12. I am as free as the wind that whispers inspiration.

GENIUS THOUGHT: Why am I so free?

_____
_____
_____
_____
_____
_____
_____

GENIUS ACTION: What action step is required of me to make this affirmation a maximized reality?

_____
_____
_____
_____
_____
_____
_____

13. The beauty of the heavens is reflected on my face.

GENIUS THOUGHT: Why is the beauty of the heavens reflected on my face?

_____
_____
_____
_____
_____
_____
_____

GENIUS ACTION: What action step is required of me to make this affirmation a maximized reality?

_____
_____
_____
_____
_____
_____
_____

14. I possess the testicular fortitude to act on behalf of those that cannot or choose not to act for themselves.

GENIUS THOUGHT: Why do I act on behalf of those that do not act for themselves?

_____
_____
_____
_____
_____
_____

GENIUS ACTION: What action step is required of me to make this affirmation a maximized reality?

_____
_____
_____
_____
_____
_____

15. The hands that I have are gifts to build monuments of excellence.

GENIUS THOUGHT: Why do I build monuments of excellence?

_____
_____
_____
_____
_____
_____
_____

GENIUS ACTION: What action step is required of me to make this affirmation a maximized reality?

_____
_____
_____
_____
_____
_____
_____

16. My children will serve as catalysts to ingenuity.

GENIUS THOUGHT: Why are my children the catalysts to my ingenuity?

_____
_____
_____
_____
_____
_____
_____

GENIUS ACTION: What action step is required of me to make this affirmation a maximized reality?

_____
_____
_____
_____
_____
_____
_____

17. I am an angel with wings of truth and honor.

GENIUS THOUGHT: Why am I an angel with wings of truth and honor?

_____
_____
_____
_____
_____
_____
_____

GENIUS ACTION: What action step is required of me to make this affirmation a maximized reality?

_____
_____
_____
_____
_____
_____
_____

18. A life of joy and prosperity is what I am continuously blessed with.

GENIUS THOUGHT: Why do I have a life of joy and prosperity?

_____
_____
_____
_____
_____
_____
_____

GENIUS ACTION: What action step is required of me to make this affirmation a maximized reality?

_____
_____
_____
_____
_____
_____
_____

19. My stride is upright and royal and negativity is beneath me.

GENIUS THOUGHT: Why is negativity beneath me?

_____
_____
_____
_____
_____
_____
_____

GENIUS ACTION: What action step is required of me to make this affirmation a maximized reality?

_____
_____
_____
_____
_____
_____
_____

20. I possess overflowing talents.

GENIUS THOUGHT: Why do I possess overflowing talents?

_____
_____
_____
_____
_____
_____
_____

GENIUS ACTION: What action step is required of me to make this affirmation a maximized reality?

_____
_____
_____
_____
_____
_____
_____

21. I realize and accept that forgiveness soothes my soul.

GENIUS THOUGHT: Why does forgiveness soothe my soul?

_____
_____
_____
_____
_____
_____
_____

GENIUS ACTION: What action step is required of me to make this affirmation a maximized reality?

_____
_____
_____
_____
_____
_____
_____

22. My actions are iconic.

GENIUS THOUGHT: Why are my actions iconic?

_____
_____
_____
_____
_____
_____

GENIUS ACTION: What action step is required of me to make this affirmation a maximized reality?

_____
_____
_____
_____
_____
_____

23. With my dance I hypnotize masses and value my rhythm.

GENIUS THOUGHT: Why is my rhythm valuable?

_____
_____
_____
_____
_____
_____

GENIUS ACTION: What action step is required of me to make this affirmation a maximized reality?

_____
_____
_____
_____
_____
_____

24. I am too intentional to become a statistic.

GENIUS THOUGHT: Why am I intentional about not becoming a statistic?

_____
_____
_____
_____
_____
_____
_____

GENIUS ACTION: What action step is required of me to make this affirmation a maximized reality?

_____
_____
_____
_____
_____
_____
_____

25. I am gifted to see a barren land and transform it into an oasis of opportunity.

GENIUS THOUGHT: Why can I transform barren lands into oasis of opportunities?

_____
_____
_____
_____
_____
_____
_____

GENIUS ACTION: What action step is required of me to make this affirmation a maximized reality?

_____
_____
_____
_____
_____
_____
_____

26. I walk in my very own definition of who I am.

GENIUS THOUGHT: Why do I walk in my definition of who I am?

_____
_____
_____
_____
_____
_____
_____

GENIUS ACTION: What action step is required of me to make this affirmation a maximized reality?

_____
_____
_____
_____
_____
_____
_____

27. My eyes are intriguing with a passion marinated by centuries.

GENIUS THOUGHT: Why are my eyes intrigued with passion?

_____
_____
_____
_____
_____
_____
_____

GENIUS ACTION: What action step is required of me to make this affirmation a maximized reality?

_____
_____
_____
_____
_____
_____
_____

28. I shall do what I fear so fear may disappear.

GENIUS THOUGHT: Why should I do what I fear?

_____
_____
_____
_____
_____
_____
_____

GENIUS ACTION: What action step is required of me to make this affirmation a maximized reality?

_____
_____
_____
_____
_____
_____
_____

29. My existence is the solution, not the problem.

GENIUS THOUGHT: Why is my existence the solution?

_____
_____
_____
_____
_____
_____
_____

GENIUS ACTION: What action step is required of me to make this affirmation a maximized reality?

_____
_____
_____
_____
_____
_____
_____

30. My spirit soars as I fly through the storm of anger.

GENIUS THOUGHT: Why does my spirit soar?

_____
_____
_____
_____
_____
_____
_____

GENIUS ACTION: What action step is required of me to make this affirmation a maximized reality?

_____
_____
_____
_____
_____
_____
_____

31. I am better than enough—I am me!

GENIUS THOUGHT: Why am I better than enough?

_____
_____
_____
_____
_____
_____

GENIUS ACTION: What action step is required of me to make this affirmation a maximized reality?

_____
_____
_____
_____
_____
_____
_____

32. My successes are too loud for ridicule to persist.

GENIUS THOUGHT: Why are my successes so loud?

_____
_____
_____
_____
_____
_____

GENIUS ACTION: What action step is required of me to make this affirmation a maximized reality?

_____
_____
_____
_____
_____
_____

33. My tongue has been refined in truth, kindness and understanding.

GENIUS THOUGHT: Why is my tongue refined in truth, kindness, and understanding?

_____
_____
_____
_____
_____
_____
_____

GENIUS ACTION: What action step is required of me to make this affirmation a maximized reality?

_____
_____
_____
_____
_____
_____
_____

34. I am sought out for my wisdom.

GENIUS THOUGHT: Why am I sought out for my wisdom?

_____
_____
_____
_____
_____
_____
_____

GENIUS ACTION: What action step is required of me to make this affirmation a maximized reality?

_____
_____
_____
_____
_____
_____
_____

35. My past is a story about me rather than my totality.

GENIUS THOUGHT: Why is my past not my totality?

_____
_____
_____
_____
_____
_____
_____

GENIUS ACTION: What action step is required of me to make this affirmation a maximized reality?

_____
_____
_____
_____
_____
_____
_____

36. God is proud of me.

GENIUS THOUGHT: Why is God proud of me?

_____
_____
_____
_____
_____
_____

GENIUS ACTION: What action step is required of me to make this affirmation a maximized reality?

_____
_____
_____
_____
_____
_____

37. I am proud of me.

GENIUS THOUGHT: Why am I proud of me?

_____
_____
_____
_____
_____
_____
_____

GENIUS ACTION: What action step is required of me to make this affirmation a maximized reality?

_____
_____
_____
_____
_____
_____
_____

38. My attitude prepares me for my altitude.

GENIUS THOUGHT: What is my attitude preparing me for?

_____
_____
_____
_____
_____
_____
_____

GENIUS ACTION: What action step is required of me to make this affirmation a maximized reality?

_____
_____
_____
_____
_____
_____
_____

39. The universe works on my behalf.

GENIUS THOUGHT: Why does the universe work on my behalf?

_____
_____
_____
_____
_____
_____
_____

GENIUS ACTION: What action step is required of me to make this affirmation a maximized reality?

_____
_____
_____
_____
_____
_____
_____

40. I am dependent upon faith alone.

GENIUS THOUGHT: Why am I dependent on faith?

_____
_____
_____
_____
_____
_____
_____

GENIUS ACTION: What action step is required of me to make this affirmation a maximized reality?

_____
_____
_____
_____
_____
_____
_____

41. My future is bright.

GENIUS THOUGHT: Why is my future so bright?

_____
_____
_____
_____
_____
_____
_____

GENIUS ACTION: What action step is required of me to make this affirmation a maximized reality?

_____
_____
_____
_____
_____
_____
_____

42. I know that I am loved.

GENIUS THOUGHT: Why am I loved?

_____
_____
_____
_____
_____
_____
_____

GENIUS ACTION: What action step is required of me to make this affirmation a maximized reality?

_____
_____
_____
_____
_____
_____
_____

43. I love me.

GENIUS THOUGHT: Why do I love me?

_____
_____
_____
_____
_____
_____

GENIUS ACTION: What action step is required of me to make this affirmation a maximized reality?

_____
_____
_____
_____
_____
_____
_____

44. I produce quality.

GENIUS THOUGHT: Why do I produce quality?

_____
_____
_____
_____
_____
_____
_____

GENIUS ACTION: What action step is required of me to make this affirmation a maximized reality?

_____
_____
_____
_____
_____
_____
_____

45. Leadership resides in me and is shown as I serve others.

GENIUS THOUGHT: What can I do since leadership resides in me?

_____
_____
_____
_____
_____
_____
_____

GENIUS ACTION: What action step is required of me to make this affirmation a maximized reality?

_____
_____
_____
_____
_____
_____
_____

46. I am a valuable person and a joy to know.

GENIUS THOUGHT: Why am I a valuable person?

_____
_____
_____
_____
_____
_____
_____

GENIUS ACTION: What action step is required of me to make this affirmation a maximized reality?

_____
_____
_____
_____
_____
_____
_____

47. My relationships are nurturing and allow me to grow in love.

GENIUS THOUGHT: How do my relationships allow me to grow in love?

_____
_____
_____
_____
_____
_____
_____

GENIUS ACTION: What action step is required of me to make this affirmation a maximized reality?

_____
_____
_____
_____
_____
_____
_____

48. I possess all of the ingredients of a successful man.

GENIUS THOUGHT: What ingredients do I possess that make me a successful man?

_____
_____
_____
_____
_____
_____
_____

GENIUS ACTION: What action step is required of me to make this affirmation a maximized reality?

_____
_____
_____
_____
_____
_____
_____

49. The friends in my life shower me with support and improve my life.

GENIUS THOUGHT: How do my friends improve my life?

_____
_____
_____
_____
_____
_____
_____

GENIUS ACTION: What action step is required of me to make this affirmation a maximized reality?

_____
_____
_____
_____
_____
_____
_____

50. Today, I am the essence of all things great.

GENIUS THOUGHT: Why am I the essence of all things great?

_____
_____
_____
_____
_____
_____
_____

GENIUS ACTION: What action step is required of me to make this affirmation a maximized reality?

_____
_____
_____
_____
_____
_____
_____

51. My business is thriving and gives me the opportunity to live financially and spiritually abundant.

GENIUS THOUGHT: Why is my business thriving?

_____
_____
_____
_____
_____
_____
_____

GENIUS ACTION: What action step is required of me to make this affirmation a maximized reality?

_____
_____
_____
_____
_____
_____
_____

52. Creativity enters my active mind continuously and through this I can change the world.

GENIUS THOUGHT: How can I change the world through my creativity?

_____
_____
_____
_____
_____
_____
_____

GENIUS ACTION: What action step is required of me to make this affirmation a maximized reality?

_____
_____
_____
_____
_____
_____
_____

53. I am the infinite possibility of all things that ever manifested or ever will be.

GENIUS THOUGHT: Why are my possibilities infinite?

_____
_____
_____
_____
_____
_____
_____

GENIUS ACTION: What action step is required of me to make this affirmation a maximized reality?

_____
_____
_____
_____
_____
_____
_____

54. My complexion is a gift and a birthright of divine intelligence.

GENIUS THOUGHT: Why is my complexion a gift?

_____
_____
_____
_____
_____
_____
_____

GENIUS ACTION: What action step is required of me to make this affirmation a maximized reality?

_____
_____
_____
_____
_____
_____
_____

55. Any challenge that I encounter is conquerable.

GENIUS THOUGHT: Why can I conquer any challenge?

_____
_____
_____
_____
_____
_____
_____

GENIUS ACTION: What action step is required of me to make this affirmation a maximized reality?

_____
_____
_____
_____
_____
_____
_____

56. My clothes are stylish because I am the most valuable thing in them.

GENIUS THOUGHT: How am I more valuable than my clothes?

___

GENIUS ACTION: What action step is required of me to make this affirmation a maximized reality?

___

57. I am the chief in my village and it is blessed because I make it so.

GENIUS THOUGHT: Why am I the chief in my village?

_____
_____
_____
_____
_____
_____
_____

GENIUS ACTION: What action step is required of me to make this affirmation a maximized reality?

_____
_____
_____
_____
_____
_____
_____

58. I have a reason to laugh and am able to bless others daily through laughter.

GENIUS THOUGHT: How is my laughter a blessing?

_____
_____
_____
_____
_____
_____

GENIUS ACTION: What action step is required of me to make this affirmation a maximized reality?

_____
_____
_____
_____
_____
_____

59. I am employable and every organization desires to pay me for my skills.

GENIUS THOUGHT: Why am I employable?

GENIUS ACTION: What action step is required of me to make this affirmation a maximized reality?

60. My lover loves me the way I am.

GENIUS THOUGHT: Why does my lover love me?

_____
_____
_____
_____
_____
_____
_____

GENIUS ACTION: What action step is required of me to make this affirmation a maximized reality?

_____
_____
_____
_____
_____
_____
_____

61. I am courageous.

GENIUS THOUGHT: How am I courageous?

_____
_____
_____
_____
_____
_____

GENIUS ACTION: What action step is required of me to make this affirmation a maximized reality?

_____
_____
_____
_____
_____
_____

62. I am admired for my style, my charisma, my brilliance and my ability.

GENIUS THOUGHT: Why am I admired?

_____
_____
_____
_____
_____
_____
_____

GENIUS ACTION: What action step is required of me to make this affirmation a maximized reality?

_____
_____
_____
_____
_____
_____
_____

63. Today I demolish thoughts that do not serve me.

GENIUS THOUGHT: What thoughts are not serving me?

_____
_____
_____
_____
_____
_____
_____

GENIUS ACTION: What action step is required of me to make this affirmation a maximized reality?

_____
_____
_____
_____
_____
_____
_____

64. I am worthy of love.

GENIUS THOUGHT: Why am I worth of love?

_____
_____
_____
_____
_____
_____
_____

GENIUS ACTION: What action step is required of me to make this affirmation a maximized reality?

_____
_____
_____
_____
_____
_____
_____

65. My future is a paradise of possibilities that I build with my thoughts and actions.

GENIUS THOUGHT: Why is paradise in my future?

_____
_____
_____
_____
_____
_____

GENIUS ACTION: What action step is required of me to make this affirmation a maximized reality?

_____
_____
_____
_____
_____
_____

66. Today I will live and thrive in the present moment.

GENIUS THOUGHT: Why live in the present moment?

_____
_____
_____
_____
_____
_____

GENIUS ACTION: What action step is required of me to make this affirmation a maximized reality?

_____
_____
_____
_____
_____
_____

67. My lips are sacred and drenched with passion.

GENIUS THOUGHT: Why are my lips sacred?

_____
_____
_____
_____
_____
_____
_____

GENIUS ACTION: What action step is required of me to make this affirmation a maximized reality?

_____
_____
_____
_____
_____
_____
_____

68. My dreams are manifested with every step of these golden feet.

GENIUS THOUGHT: How are my dreams manifested?

_____
_____
_____
_____
_____
_____
_____

GENIUS ACTION: What action step is required of me to make this affirmation a maximized reality?

_____
_____
_____
_____
_____
_____
_____

69. I show the bliss of what it is to be sun-kissed and free.

GENIUS THOUGHT: Why am I free?

_____
_____
_____
_____
_____
_____
_____

GENIUS ACTION: What action step is required of me to make this affirmation a maximized reality?

_____
_____
_____
_____
_____
_____
_____

70. My fears are overcome by my tenacity.

GENIUS THOUGHT: Why have I overcome my fears?

_____
_____
_____
_____
_____
_____
_____

GENIUS ACTION: What action step is required of me to make this affirmation a maximized reality?

_____
_____
_____
_____
_____
_____
_____

71. I am blessed.

GENIUS THOUGHT: Why am I blessed?

_____
_____
_____
_____
_____
_____
_____

GENIUS ACTION: What action step is required of me to make this affirmation a maximized reality?

_____
_____
_____
_____
_____
_____
_____

72. My moment is now.

GENIUS THOUGHT: Why is now my moment?

_____
_____
_____
_____
_____
_____
_____

GENIUS ACTION: What action step is required of me to make this affirmation a maximized reality?

_____
_____
_____
_____
_____
_____
_____

73. The world is my playground.

GENIUS THOUGHT: How is the world my playground?

_____
_____
_____
_____
_____
_____
_____

GENIUS ACTION: What action step is required of me to make this affirmation a maximized reality?

_____
_____
_____
_____
_____
_____
_____

74. My life is filled with meaning and opportunity.

GENIUS THOUGHT: Why is my life filled with meaning?

_____
_____
_____
_____
_____
_____
_____

GENIUS ACTION: What action step is required of me to make this affirmation a maximized reality?

_____
_____
_____
_____
_____
_____
_____

75. My skin is the miracle of life.

GENIUS THOUGHT: Why is my skin miraculous?

_____
_____
_____
_____
_____
_____
_____

GENIUS ACTION: What action step is required of me to make this affirmation a maximized reality?

_____
_____
_____
_____
_____
_____
_____

76. Any rejection in my life is only redirection to live a better life.

GENIUS THOUGHT: Why are my rejections actually redirections?

_____
_____
_____
_____
_____
_____
_____

GENIUS ACTION: What action step is required of me to make this affirmation a maximized reality?

_____
_____
_____
_____
_____
_____
_____

77. I was built for the responsibility of manhood.

GENIUS THOUGHT: Why was I built for manhood?

___

GENIUS ACTION: What action step is required of me to make this affirmation a maximized reality?

___

78. I radiate a healthy lifestyle and reap the benefits of wellness.

GENIUS THOUGHT: How do I reap the benefits of wellness?

_____
_____
_____
_____
_____
_____
_____

GENIUS ACTION: What action step is required of me to make this affirmation a maximized reality?

_____
_____
_____
_____
_____
_____
_____

79. The perfect romantic partner for me is alive, well and pursuing their dreams.

GENIUS THOUGHT: Why is my partner pursuing their dreams?

_____
_____
_____
_____
_____
_____
_____

GENIUS ACTION: What action step is required of me to make this affirmation a maximized reality?

_____
_____
_____
_____
_____
_____
_____

80. Any obstacle I encounter is nourishment for my greatness.

GENIUS THOUGHT: How do obstacles nourish my greatness?

_____
_____
_____
_____
_____
_____
_____

GENIUS ACTION: What action step is required of me to make this affirmation a maximized reality?

_____
_____
_____
_____
_____
_____
_____

81. I honor my spirit by digesting positivity and bathing in awareness.

GENIUS THOUGHT: Why does my spirit digest positivity?

_____
_____
_____
_____
_____
_____
_____

GENIUS ACTION. What action step is required of me to make this affirmation a maximized reality?

_____
_____
_____
_____
_____
_____
_____

82. I honor those who are no longer with me by feeling the vibrations of their spirits.

GENIUS THOUGHT: Why do I honor those who are no longer with me?

_____
_____
_____
_____
_____
_____
_____

GENIUS ACTION: What action step is required of me to make this affirmation a maximized reality?

_____
_____
_____
_____
_____
_____
_____

83. My inner light is a source of strength that grows daily.

GENIUS THOUGHT: How does my strength grow daily?

_____
_____
_____
_____
_____
_____
_____

GENIUS ACTION. What action step is required of me to make this affirmation a maximized reality?

_____
_____
_____
_____
_____
_____
_____

84. I am the product of over one million sources of cosmic consciousness.

GENIUS THOUGHT: How am I a product of consciousness?

_____
_____
_____
_____
_____
_____

GENIUS ACTION: What action step is required of me to make this affirmation a maximized reality?

_____
_____
_____
_____
_____
_____

85. My past serves to make me better instead of bitter.

GENIUS THOUGHT: How am I better because of my past?

_____
_____
_____
_____
_____
_____

GENIUS ACTION: What action step is required of me to make this affirmation a maximized reality?

_____
_____
_____
_____
_____
_____

86. My aura is drenched in ambition.

GENIUS THOUGHT: Why am I drenched in ambition?

_____
_____
_____
_____
_____
_____

GENIUS ACTION: What action step is required of me to make this affirmation a maximized reality?

_____
_____
_____
_____
_____
_____
_____

87. All of my answers lie within the treasure chest of my soul.

GENIUS THOUGHT: How do my answers lie within?

GENIUS ACTION. What action step is required of me to make this affirmation a maximized reality?

88. I know that today will be as handsome as I am.

GENIUS THOUGHT: Why does today look so good?

_____
_____
_____
_____
_____
_____
_____

GENIUS ACTION: What action step is required of me to make this affirmation a maximized reality?

_____
_____
_____
_____
_____
_____
_____

89. My money and financial accounts work for me and create paths to wealth.

GENIUS THOUGHT: How does my money work for me?

_____
_____
_____
_____
_____
_____
_____

GENIUS ACTION. What action step is required of me to make this affirmation a maximized reality?

_____
_____
_____
_____
_____
_____
_____

90. My vision is lit with clarity.

GENIUS THOUGHT: Why is my vision clear?

_____
_____
_____
_____
_____
_____
_____

GENIUS ACTION: What action step is required of me to make this affirmation a maximized reality?

_____
_____
_____
_____
_____
_____
_____

91. Life is lived superbly with every breath.

GENIUS THOUGHT: Why is my life superb?

_____
_____
_____
_____
_____
_____
_____

GENIUS ACTION: What action step is required of me to make this affirmation a maximized reality?

_____
_____
_____
_____
_____
_____
_____

92. I am raising my child (ren) on purpose.

GENIUS THOUGHT: Why am I raising my child (ren) on purpose?

_____
_____
_____
_____
_____
_____
_____

GENIUS ACTION: What action step is required of me to make this affirmation a maximized reality?

_____
_____
_____
_____
_____
_____
_____

93. My family unit loves one another unconditionally.

GENIUS THOUGHT: Why does my family love me unconditionally?

_____
_____
_____
_____
_____
_____
_____

GENIUS ACTION: What action step is required of me to make this affirmation a maximized reality?

_____
_____
_____
_____
_____
_____
_____

94. I honor diversity in the universe.

GENIUS THOUGHT: How do I honor diversity?

_____
_____
_____
_____
_____
_____

GENIUS ACTION: What action step is required of me to make this affirmation a maximized reality?

_____
_____
_____
_____
_____
_____

95. I honor my authentic self by surrounding myself with love and respect.

GENIUS THOUGHT: Why do I surround myself with love and respect?

_____
_____
_____
_____
_____
_____
_____

GENIUS ACTION: What action step is required of me to make this affirmation a maximized reality?

_____
_____
_____
_____
_____
_____
_____

96. I am amazing.

GENIUS THOUGHT: Why am I amazing?

_____
_____
_____
_____
_____
_____

GENIUS ACTION: What action step is required of me to make this affirmation a maximized reality?

_____
_____
_____
_____
_____
_____

97. The potential within is limitless by my thoughts.

GENIUS THOUGHT: How is my potential limitless?

_____
_____
_____
_____
_____
_____
_____

GENIUS ACTION: What action step is required of me to make this affirmation a maximized reality?

_____
_____
_____
_____
_____
_____
_____

98. My five senses perceive every experience with love.

GENIUS THOUGHT: Why do I perceive with love?

GENIUS ACTION: What action step is required of me to make this affirmation a maximized reality?

99. All is well.

GENIUS THOUGHT: Why is all well?

_____
_____
_____
_____
_____
_____
_____

GENIUS ACTION: What action step is required of me to make this affirmation a maximized reality?

_____
_____
_____
_____
_____
_____
_____

100. I am surrounded, consumed, adorned and enthralled by miracles.

GENIUS THOUGHT: Why am I surrounded by miracles?

_____
_____
_____
_____
_____
_____
_____

GENIUS ACTION: What action step is required of me to make this affirmation a maximized reality?

_____
_____
_____
_____
_____
_____
_____

101. All that I desire comes in perfect timing.

GENIUS THOUGHT: Why do my desires come in perfect timing?

_____
_____
_____
_____
_____
_____
_____

GENIUS ACTION: What action step is required of me to make this affirmation a maximized reality?

_____
_____
_____
_____
_____
_____
_____

102. I have more to offer the world than sexuality and criticism.

GENIUS THOUGHT: What more to I have to offer to the world?

_____
_____
_____
_____
_____
_____

GENIUS ACTION: What action step is required of me to make this affirmation a maximized reality?

_____
_____
_____
_____
_____
_____

103. My team is filled with thoughtful individuals that want the best for me.

GENIUS THOUGHT: Why does my team want the best for me?

_____
_____
_____
_____
_____
_____
_____

GENIUS ACTION: What action step is required of me to make this affirmation a maximized reality?

_____
_____
_____
_____
_____
_____
_____

104. I let go of what desires to destroy my legacy and me.

GENIUS THOUGHT: How do I let go of what wants to destroy me?

_____
_____
_____
_____
_____
_____
_____

GENIUS ACTION: What action step is required of me to make this affirmation a maximized reality?

_____
_____
_____
_____
_____
_____
_____

105. My body is a physical manifestation of awesome.

GENIUS THOUGHT: Why is my body awesome?

_____
_____
_____
_____
_____
_____
_____

GENIUS ACTION: What action step is required of me to make this affirmation a maximized reality?

_____
_____
_____
_____
_____
_____
_____

106. The universe conspires new exciting ways to behold my life.

GENIUS THOUGHT: How does the universe conspire on my life?

_____
_____
_____
_____
_____
_____
_____

GENIUS ACTION: What action step is required of me to make this affirmation a maximized reality?

_____
_____
_____
_____
_____
_____
_____

107. I am more than what my past has revealed.

GENIUS THOUGHT: Why am I more than my past?

GENIUS ACTION: What action step is required of me to make this affirmation a maximized reality?

108. I am grateful.

GENIUS THOUGHT: Why am I grateful?

GENIUS ACTION: What action step is required of me to make this affirmation a maximized reality?

109. My happiness is contagious and creates a force field of positive energy.

GENIUS THOUGHT: How is my happiness contagious?

_____
_____
_____
_____
_____
_____
_____

GENIUS ACTION: What action step is required of me to make this affirmation a maximized reality?

_____
_____
_____
_____
_____
_____
_____

110. I operate in forgiveness by first forgiving myself.

GENIUS THOUGHT: How do I forgive myself?

_____
_____
_____
_____
_____
_____
_____

GENIUS ACTION: What action step is required of me to make this affirmation a maximized reality?

_____
_____
_____
_____
_____
_____
_____

111. I awake daily to a wonderful life.

GENIUS THOUGHT: Why do I awake to a wonderful life?

_____
_____
_____
_____
_____
_____
_____

GENIUS ACTION: What action step is required of me to make this affirmation a maximized reality?

_____
_____
_____
_____
_____
_____
_____

112. I reside in moments of glory.

GENIUS THOUGHT: Why do I reside in moments of glory?

_____
_____
_____
_____
_____
_____
_____

GENIUS ACTION: What action step is required of me to make this affirmation a maximized reality?

_____
_____
_____
_____
_____
_____
_____

113. I look forward to laughing with all teeth and tonsils.

GENIUS THOUGHT: Why do I laugh with all teeth and tonsils?

_____
_____
_____
_____
_____
_____

GENIUS ACTION: What action step is required of me to make this affirmation a maximized reality?

_____
_____
_____
_____
_____
_____

114. I will close the doors that lead me to nowhere.

GENIUS THOUGHT: How will I close doors to nowhere?

_____
_____
_____
_____
_____
_____
_____

GENIUS ACTION: What action step is required of me to make this affirmation a maximized reality?

_____
_____
_____
_____
_____
_____
_____

115. Today will be embraced like a dear friend.

GENIUS THOUGHT: Why will I embrace today?

_____
_____
_____
_____
_____
_____
_____

GENIUS ACTION: What action step is required of me to make this affirmation a maximized reality?

_____
_____
_____
_____
_____
_____
_____

116. The shade of me that I see requires no change, only praise.

GENIUS THOUGHT: How will I praise my shade?

_____
_____
_____
_____
_____
_____
_____

GENIUS ACTION: What action step is required of me to make this affirmation a maximized reality?

_____
_____
_____
_____
_____
_____
_____

117. I am open to receive love and affection.

GENIUS THOUGHT: Why am I open to receive love and affection?

_____
_____
_____
_____
_____
_____
_____

GENIUS ACTION: What action step is required of me to make this affirmation a maximized reality?

_____
_____
_____
_____
_____
_____
_____

118. I am the best version of myself.

GENIUS THOUGHT: Why am I the best version of me?

_____
_____
_____
_____
_____
_____
_____

GENIUS ACTION: What action step is required of me to make this affirmation a maximized reality?

_____
_____
_____
_____
_____
_____
_____

119. Change works in my favor.

GENIUS THOUGHT: How does change work for me?

_____
_____
_____
_____
_____
_____
_____

GENIUS ACTION: What action step is required of me to make this affirmation a maximized reality?

_____
_____
_____
_____
_____
_____
_____

120. I am a product of grace and I give as I am.

GENIUS THOUGHT: Why am I a product of grace?

_____
_____
_____
_____
_____
_____
_____

GENIUS ACTION: What action step is required of me to make this affirmation a maximized reality?

_____
_____
_____
_____
_____
_____
_____

121. All I require is me.

GENIUS THOUGHT: Why am I all that I require?

_____
_____
_____
_____
_____
_____
_____

GENIUS ACTION: What action step is required of me to make this affirmation a maximized reality?

_____
_____
_____
_____
_____
_____
_____

123. There is no competition because I am the standard for my life.

GENIUS THOUGHT: How is there no competition?

_____
_____
_____
_____
_____
_____

GENIUS ACTION: What action step is required of me to make this affirmation a maximized reality?

_____
_____
_____
_____
_____
_____

124. My inner peace molds my existence.

GENIUS THOUGHT: How does my inner peace mold my existence?

_____
_____
_____
_____
_____
_____
_____

GENIUS ACTION: What action step is required of me to make this affirmation a maximized reality?

_____
_____
_____
_____
_____
_____
_____

125. Today I remove the painful thorns of my past in an effort to experience the bouquet of life.

GENIUS THOUGHT: How do I remove the painful thorns of my past?

_____
_____
_____
_____
_____
_____
_____

GENIUS ACTION: What action step is required of me to make this affirmation a maximized reality?

_____
_____
_____
_____
_____
_____
_____

126. My culture does not restrain me but allows me to dream in color.

GENIUS THOUGHT: How does my culture not restrain me?

_____
_____
_____
_____
_____
_____
_____

GENIUS ACTION. What action step is required of me to make this affirmation a maximized reality?

_____
_____
_____
_____
_____
_____
_____

127. I am intellectually subservient to no one.

GENIUS THOUGHT: Why am I not subservient to anyone?

GENIUS ACTION: What action step is required of me to make this affirmation a maximized reality?

128. I can make a dollar out of 15¢ and $1 million from a thought.

GENIUS THOUGHT: How can I make money from a thought?

GENIUS ACTION: What action step is required of me to make this affirmation a maximized reality?

129. I honor the divinity that resides in me.

GENIUS THOUGHT: How do I honor the divinity in me?

_____
_____
_____
_____
_____
_____
_____

GENIUS ACTION: What action step is required of me to make this affirmation a maximized reality?

_____
_____
_____
_____
_____
_____
_____

130. The only approval I search for is my own.

GENIUS THOUGHT: Why is my approval important?

_____
_____
_____
_____
_____
_____
_____

GENIUS ACTION: What action step is required of me to make this affirmation a maximized reality?

_____
_____
_____
_____
_____
_____
_____

131. When I open my mouth, lions and peacocks join in strengthened beauty.

GENIUS THOUGHT: What do I say that is strengthened beauty?

___

GENIUS ACTION: What action step is required of me to make this affirmation a maximized reality?

___

132. I am the perfect chord in the song of life.

GENIUS THOUGHT: Why am I the perfect chord?

_____
_____
_____
_____
_____
_____
_____

GENIUS ACTION: What action step is required of me to make this affirmation a maximized reality?

_____
_____
_____
_____
_____
_____
_____

133. Relaxation is a part of my everyday activity.

GENIUS THOUGHT: Why should I relax?

_____
_____
_____
_____
_____
_____
_____

GENIUS ACTION: What action step is required of me to make this affirmation a maximized reality?

_____
_____
_____
_____
_____
_____
_____

134. Prosperity has become my new normal.

GENIUS THOUGHT: Why is prosperity my new normal?

_____
_____
_____
_____
_____
_____
_____

GENIUS ACTION: What action step is required of me to make this affirmation a maximized reality?

_____
_____
_____
_____
_____
_____
_____

135. The work I perform daily allows me to create my ladder of success.

GENIUS THOUGHT: How do I create a ladder of success?

_____
_____
_____
_____
_____
_____

GENIUS ACTION: What action step is required of me to make this affirmation a maximized reality?

_____
_____
_____
_____
_____
_____

136. Worry is no longer a part of my agenda; my imagination has been put to better use.

GENIUS THOUGHT: How do I use my imagination?

_____
_____
_____
_____
_____
_____
_____

GENIUS ACTION: What action step is required of me to make this affirmation a maximized reality?

_____
_____
_____
_____
_____
_____
_____

137. I stand for my convictions.

GENIUS THOUGHT: How do I stand for my convictions?

_____
_____
_____
_____
_____
_____
_____

GENIUS ACTION: What action step is required of me to make this affirmation a maximized reality?

_____
_____
_____
_____
_____
_____
_____

138. I possess an unconquerable element of adaptability.

GENIUS THOUGHT: Why am I adaptable?

GENIUS ACTION: What action step is required of me to make this affirmation a maximized reality?

139. I attract money effortlessly.

GENIUS THOUGHT: Why do I attract money?

_____
_____
_____
_____
_____
_____
_____

GENIUS ACTION: What action step is required of me to make this affirmation a maximized reality?

_____
_____
_____
_____
_____
_____
_____

140. I am responsive to possibilities that position me to greatness.

GENIUS THOUGHT: How am I responsive to possibilities?

_____
_____
_____
_____
_____
_____
_____

GENIUS ACTION: What action step is required of me to make this affirmation a maximized reality?

_____
_____
_____
_____
_____
_____
_____

141. I am thankful that money has decided to work for me.

GENIUS THOUGHT: How does money work for me?

_____
_____
_____
_____
_____
_____

GENIUS ACTION: What action step is required of me to make this affirmation a maximized reality?

_____
_____
_____
_____
_____
_____

142. I exude power.

GENIUS THOUGHT: How do I exude power?

GENIUS ACTION: What action step is required of me to make this affirmation a maximized reality?

143. I am guided by divinity with every passing second.

GENIUS THOUGHT: Why am I guided by divinity?

_____
_____
_____
_____
_____
_____
_____

GENIUS ACTION: What action step is required of me to make this affirmation a maximized reality?

_____
_____
_____
_____
_____
_____
_____

144. My home is my sanctuary where peace and tranquility abide.

GENIUS THOUGHT: Why is my home filled with peace and tranquility?

_____
_____
_____
_____
_____
_____
_____

GENIUS ACTION: What action step is required of me to make this affirmation a maximized reality?

_____
_____
_____
_____
_____
_____
_____

145. I honor all of my God-given abilities.

GENIUS THOUGHT: How do I honor my abilities?

_____
_____
_____
_____
_____
_____
_____

GENIUS ACTION: What action step is required of me to make this affirmation a maximized reality?

_____
_____
_____
_____
_____
_____
_____

146. Yes, I can.

GENIUS THOUGHT: How can I?

___

GENIUS ACTION: What action step is required of me to make this affirmation a maximized reality?

___

147. I have the audacity to make it all better.

GENIUS THOUGHT: How can I make it better?

_____
_____
_____
_____
_____
_____

GENIUS ACTION: What action step is required of me to make this affirmation a maximized reality?

_____
_____
_____
_____
_____
_____

148. My optimism is priceless.

GENIUS THOUGHT: Why is my optimism priceless?

_____
_____
_____
_____
_____
_____
_____

GENIUS ACTION: What action step is required of me to make this affirmation a maximized reality?

_____
_____
_____
_____
_____
_____
_____

149. I am honored to see heaven on earth.

GENIUS THOUGHT: How do I see heaven on earth?

_____
_____
_____
_____
_____
_____
_____

GENIUS ACTION: What action step is required of me to make this affirmation a maximized reality?

_____
_____
_____
_____
_____
_____
_____

150. I am happy.

GENIUS THOUGHT: Why am I happy?

_____
_____
_____
_____
_____
_____
_____

GENIUS ACTION: What action step is required of me to make this affirmation a maximized reality?

_____
_____
_____
_____
_____
_____
_____

151. My romantic notions are intoxicating.

GENIUS THOUGHT: How are my romantic notions intoxicating?

_____

GENIUS ACTION: What action step is required of me to make this affirmation a maximized reality?

_____

152. The rest of my life will be the best of my life.

GENIUS THOUGHT: How will the rest of my life be the best of my life?

_____
_____
_____
_____
_____
_____
_____

GENIUS ACTION: What action step is required of me to make this affirmation a maximized reality?

_____
_____
_____
_____
_____
_____
_____

153. I am worth knowing so I will study to master myself.

GENIUS THOUGHT: How will I study to master myself?

_____
_____
_____
_____
_____
_____

GENIUS ACTION: What action step is required of me to make this affirmation a maximized reality?

_____
_____
_____
_____
_____
_____

154. I am the luckiest person I know.

GENIUS THOUGHT: Why am I so lucky?

_____
_____
_____
_____
_____
_____
_____

GENIUS ACTION: What action step is required of me to make this affirmation a maximized reality?

_____
_____
_____
_____
_____
_____
_____

155. I will create a life of bliss with all available tools.

GENIUS THOUGHT: Why will I create a life of bliss?

_____
_____
_____
_____
_____
_____
_____

GENIUS ACTION: What action step is required of me to make this affirmation a maximized reality?

_____
_____
_____
_____
_____
_____
_____

156. I am a force of energy that has taken the universe millenniums to create.

GENIUS THOUGHT: Why has it taken the universe millenniums to create me?

GENIUS ACTION: What action step is required of me to make this affirmation a maximized reality?

157. I shall grow my child (ren) in a field of love and creativity.

GENIUS THOUGHT: How will I grow my child (ren) in love and creativity?

_____
_____
_____
_____
_____
_____
_____

GENIUS ACTION: What action step is required of me to make this affirmation a maximized reality?

_____
_____
_____
_____
_____
_____
_____

158. I am addicted to smiling.

GENIUS THOUGHT: Why am I addicted to smiling?

_____
_____
_____
_____
_____
_____

GENIUS ACTION: What action step is required of me to make this affirmation a maximized reality?

_____
_____
_____
_____
_____
_____

159. I dare to dream out loud.

GENIUS THOUGHT: Why do I dream out loud?

_____
_____
_____
_____
_____
_____

GENIUS ACTION: What action step is required of me to make this affirmation a maximized reality?

_____
_____
_____
_____
_____
_____

160. Today I will think big.

GENIUS THOUGHT: Why do I think big?

_____
_____
_____
_____
_____
_____

GENIUS ACTION: What action step is required of me to make this affirmation a maximized reality?

_____
_____
_____
_____
_____
_____

161. I will do more of what makes me awesome.

GENIUS THOUGHT: What makes me awesome?

_____
_____
_____
_____
_____
_____

GENIUS ACTION: What action step is required of me to make this affirmation a maximized reality?

_____
_____
_____
_____
_____
_____

162. I am always on time.

GENIUS THOUGHT: Why am I always on time?

_____
_____
_____
_____
_____
_____

GENIUS ACTION: What action step is required of me to make this affirmation a maximized reality?

_____
_____
_____
_____
_____
_____

163. I am aware of my kinetic energy and my potential energy is unfathomable.

GENIUS THOUGHT: Why is my potential energy unfathomable?

_____
_____
_____
_____
_____
_____
_____

GENIUS ACTION: What action step is required of me to make this affirmation a maximized reality?

_____
_____
_____
_____
_____
_____
_____

164. I am free.

GENIUS THOUGHT: Why am I free?

_____
_____
_____
_____
_____
_____
_____

GENIUS ACTION: What action step is required of me to make this affirmation a maximized reality?

_____
_____
_____
_____
_____
_____
_____

165. I am more valuable today than I have ever been before.

GENIUS THOUGHT: How am I valuable today?

_____
_____
_____
_____
_____
_____
_____

GENIUS ACTION: What action step is required of me to make this affirmation a maximized reality?

_____
_____
_____
_____
_____
_____
_____

166. Today I will excite my spirit to align with my purpose.

GENIUS THOUGHT: How will I align my spirit to my purpose?

_____
_____
_____
_____
_____
_____
_____

GENIUS ACTION: What action step is required of me to make this affirmation a maximized reality?

_____
_____
_____
_____
_____
_____
_____

167. Giving up is not an option.

GENIUS THOUGHT: Why is giving up not an option?

___

GENIUS ACTION: What action step is required of me to make this affirmation a maximized reality?

___

168. I have greatness within me.

GENIUS THOUGHT: How do I have greatness within me?

_____
_____
_____
_____
_____
_____

GENIUS ACTION: What action step is required of me to make this affirmation a maximized reality?

_____
_____
_____
_____
_____
_____

169. I bask in being unusual.

GENIUS THOUGHT: How am I unusual?

_____
_____
_____
_____
_____
_____

GENIUS ACTION: What action step is required of me to make this affirmation a maximized reality?

_____
_____
_____
_____
_____
_____

170. I will do today what makes my soul smile.

GENIUS THOUGHT: What makes my soul smile?

_____
_____
_____
_____
_____
_____

GENIUS ACTION: What action step is required of me to make this affirmation a maximized reality?

_____
_____
_____
_____
_____
_____

171. Today I will exercise my right to make a decision.

GENIUS THOUGHT: What decision will I make today?

GENIUS ACTION: What action step is required of me to make this affirmation a maximized reality?

171. I live in a balanced state of mindfulness.

GENIUS THOUGHT: Why do I live in a balanced state of mindfulness?

___

GENIUS ACTION: What action step is required of me to make this affirmation a maximized reality?

172. I am anchored in peace.

GENIUS THOUGHT: How am I anchored in peace?

GENIUS ACTION: What action step is required of me to make this affirmation a maximized reality?

173. I come from a people processed in divine light.

GENIUS THOUGHT: Why were my people processed in divine light?

_____
_____
_____
_____
_____
_____
_____

GENIUS ACTION: What action step is required of me to make this affirmation a maximized reality?

_____
_____
_____
_____
_____
_____
_____

174. Every ripple, crevice, valley and muscle on my body was chiseled by the hand of God.

GENIUS THOUGHT: Why was my body chiseled by the hand of God?

_____
_____
_____
_____
_____
_____
_____

GENIUS ACTION: What action step is required of me to make this affirmation a maximized reality?

_____
_____
_____
_____
_____
_____
_____

175. I am infused with God thoughts that prepare my path.

GENIUS THOUGHT: Why am I infused with God thoughts?

_____
_____
_____
_____
_____
_____
_____

GENIUS ACTION: What action step is required of me to make this affirmation a maximized reality?

_____
_____
_____
_____
_____
_____
_____

176. I am at a higher state of Being than I was yesterday.

GENIUS THOUGHT: Why am I at a higher state of Being?

_____
_____
_____
_____
_____
_____
_____

GENIUS ACTION: What action step is required of me to make this affirmation a maximized reality?

_____
_____
_____
_____
_____
_____
_____

177. With each new day I am bathed in appreciation.

GENIUS THOUGHT: How am I bathed in appreciation?

_____
_____
_____
_____
_____
_____
_____

GENIUS ACTION: What action step is required of me to make this affirmation a maximized reality?

_____
_____
_____
_____
_____
_____
_____

178. I walk in the celebration of inspiration.

GENIUS THOUGHT: Why do I walk in the celebration of inspiration?

GENIUS ACTION: What action step is required of me to make this affirmation a maximized reality?

179. My communion with God is pure and adequate.

GENIUS THOUGHT: Why is my communion with God adequate?

_____
_____
_____
_____
_____
_____
_____

GENIUS ACTION: What action step is required of me to make this affirmation a maximized reality?

_____
_____
_____
_____
_____
_____
_____

180. I am dynamically and wonderfully made into a human image of beauty.

GENIUS THOUGHT: Why am I wonderfully made?

_____
_____
_____
_____
_____
_____

GENIUS ACTION: What action step is required of me to make this affirmation a maximized reality?

_____
_____
_____
_____
_____
_____

181. I alone have the power to change my emotional well-being.

GENIUS THOUGHT: How do I change my emotional well-being?

_____
_____
_____
_____
_____
_____
_____

GENIUS ACTION: What action step is required of me to make this affirmation a maximized reality?

_____
_____
_____
_____
_____
_____
_____

182. I am the imagination of myself and no one else.

GENIUS THOUGHT: How do I imagine myself?

_____
_____
_____
_____
_____
_____

GENIUS ACTION: What action step is required of me to make this affirmation a maximized reality?

_____
_____
_____
_____
_____
_____

183. The hue of my skin sends sensations of wonder, reverence, ecstasy and vitality.

GENIUS THOUGHT: How does my skin send sensations of wonder and reverence?

_____
_____
_____
_____
_____
_____
_____

GENIUS ACTION: What action step is required of me to make this affirmation a maximized reality?

_____
_____
_____
_____
_____
_____
_____

184. I operate in wholeness.

GENIUS THOUGHT: Why do I operate in wholeness?

GENIUS ACTION: What action step is required of me to make this affirmation a maximized reality?

185. I invest in myself through prayer, meditation, education and effort.

GENIUS THOUGHT: How do I invest in myself through meditation and effort?

_____
_____
_____
_____
_____
_____
_____

GENIUS ACTION: What action step is required of me to make this affirmation a maximized reality?

_____
_____
_____
_____
_____
_____
_____

186. I am better than granny's plate of collard greens and cornbread.

GENIUS THOUGHT: How am I better than a plate of food prepared by my granny?

_____
_____
_____
_____
_____
_____
_____

GENIUS ACTION: What action step is required of me to make this affirmation a maximized reality?

_____
_____
_____
_____
_____
_____
_____

187. I honor my manhood when I show my full range of emotions.

GENIUS THOUGHT: Why do I show my full range of emotions?

_____
_____
_____
_____
_____
_____
_____

GENIUS ACTION: What action step is required of me to make this affirmation a maximized reality?

_____
_____
_____
_____
_____
_____
_____

188. I acknowledge the incredible man I see in the mirror.

GENIUS THOUGHT: Why do I acknowledge the incredible man I see in the mirror?

_____
_____
_____
_____
_____
_____
_____

GENIUS ACTION: What action step is required of me to make this affirmation a maximized reality?

_____
_____
_____
_____
_____
_____
_____

189. My level of provision for my family is glorious!

GENIUS THOUGHT: How is my level of provision glorious?

_____
_____
_____
_____
_____
_____
_____

GENIUS ACTION: What action step is required of me to make this affirmation a maximized reality?

_____
_____
_____
_____
_____
_____
_____

190. I am learning to love my hair.

GENIUS THOUGHT: How am I loving my hair?

_____
_____
_____
_____
_____
_____

GENIUS ACTION: What action step is required of me to make this affirmation a maximized reality?

_____
_____
_____
_____
_____
_____

191. My connection to perfection is healed.

GENIUS THOUGHT: How am I healed from my connection to perfection?

_____
_____
_____
_____
_____
_____
_____

GENIUS ACTION: What action step is required of me to make this affirmation a maximized reality?

_____
_____
_____
_____
_____
_____
_____

192. Today I smile for the person I am becoming.

GENIUS THOUGHT: Why do I smile for the person I am becoming?

_____
_____
_____
_____
_____
_____

GENIUS ACTION: What action step is required of me to make this affirmation a maximized reality?

_____
_____
_____
_____
_____
_____

193. I am fulfilled as I express generosity.

GENIUS THOUGHT: How do I express generosity?

_____
_____
_____
_____
_____
_____
_____

GENIUS ACTION: What action step is required of me to make this affirmation a maximized reality?

_____
_____
_____
_____
_____
_____
_____

194. My heart blossoms with the presence of all that is divine.

GENIUS THOUGHT: Why does my heart blossom in the presence of divinity?

_____
_____
_____
_____
_____
_____
_____

GENIUS ACTION: What action step is required of me to make this affirmation a maximized reality?

_____
_____
_____
_____
_____
_____
_____

195. My actions inspire others to dream.

GENIUS THOUGHT: How do my actions inspire others to dream?

GENIUS ACTION: What action step is required of me to make this affirmation a maximized reality?

196. I think I am handsome, if I do say so myself.

GENIUS THOUGHT: Why do I think I am handsome?

_____
_____
_____
_____
_____
_____
_____

GENIUS ACTION: What action step is required of me to make this affirmation a maximized reality?

_____
_____
_____
_____
_____
_____
_____

197. I am above conditions.

GENIUS THOUGHT: Why am I above conditions?

_____
_____
_____
_____
_____
_____
_____

GENIUS ACTION: What action step is required of me to make this affirmation a maximized reality?

_____
_____
_____
_____
_____
_____
_____

198. I am beyond limitation.

GENIUS THOUGHT: Why am I beyond limitations?

_____
_____
_____
_____
_____
_____

GENIUS ACTION: What action step is required of me to make this affirmation a maximized reality?

_____
_____
_____
_____
_____
_____

199. I am a well of wise counsel.

GENIUS THOUGHT: How am I a well of wise counsel?

___

GENIUS ACTION: What action step is required of me to make this affirmation a maximized reality?

___

200. I am allowed to love myself more than others.

GENIUS THOUGHT: Why am I allowed to love myself more?

_____
_____
_____
_____
_____
_____
_____

GENIUS ACTION: What action step is required of me to make this affirmation a maximized reality?

_____
_____
_____
_____
_____
_____
_____

201. I am more than this beautiful man of purpose; I am a spirit having a human experience.

GENIUS THOUGHT: Why am I having a human experience?

_____
_____
_____
_____
_____
_____
_____

GENIUS ACTION: What action step is required of me to make this affirmation a maximized reality?

_____
_____
_____
_____
_____
_____
_____

202. I am only willing to expect the best in life.

GENIUS THOUGHT: Why am I willing to only expect the best?

_____
_____
_____
_____
_____
_____
_____

GENIUS ACTION: What action step is required of me to make this affirmation a maximized reality?

_____
_____
_____
_____
_____
_____
_____

203. I live to enhance the freedom of others.

GENIUS THOUGHT: Why do I enhance the freedom of others?

GENIUS ACTION: What action step is required of me to make this affirmation a maximized reality?

204. I am a goal digger.

GENIUS THOUGHT: Why am I a goal digger?

_____
_____
_____
_____
_____
_____
_____

GENIUS ACTION: What action step is required of me to make this affirmation a maximized reality?

_____
_____
_____
_____
_____
_____
_____

205. I honor my elders and their experiences.

GENIUS THOUGHT: How do I honor my elders?

_____
_____
_____
_____
_____
_____
_____

GENIUS ACTION: What action step is required of me to make this affirmation a maximized reality?

_____
_____
_____
_____
_____
_____
_____

206. I am changing my thoughts about situations in an effort to be happy.

GENIUS THOUGHT: Why am I changing my thoughts to be happy?

_____
_____
_____
_____
_____
_____
_____

GENIUS ACTION: What action step is required of me to make this affirmation a maximized reality?

_____
_____
_____
_____
_____
_____
_____

207. I am more than a collection of letters that others choose to identify me with.

GENIUS THOUGHT: How am I more than a collection letters?

_____
_____
_____
_____
_____
_____
_____

GENIUS ACTION: What action step is required of me to make this affirmation a maximized reality?

_____
_____
_____
_____
_____
_____
_____

207. I am expanding my comfort zone.

GENIUS THOUGHT: Why am I expanding my comfort zone?

_____
_____
_____
_____
_____
_____

GENIUS ACTION: What action step is required of me to make this affirmation a maximized reality?

_____
_____
_____
_____
_____
_____

208. Today will be a bright and blissful day.

GENIUS THOUGHT: How will my day be bright and blissful?

_____
_____
_____
_____
_____
_____
_____

GENIUS ACTION: What action step is required of me to make this affirmation a maximized reality?

_____
_____
_____
_____
_____
_____
_____

209. I am willing to let go.

GENIUS THOUGHT: Why am I willing to let go?

_____
_____
_____
_____
_____
_____
_____

GENIUS ACTION: What action step is required of me to make this affirmation a maximized reality?

_____
_____
_____
_____
_____
_____
_____

210. I am bigger than any problem.

GENIUS THOUGHT: Why am I bigger than my problem?

_____
_____
_____
_____
_____
_____
_____

GENIUS ACTION: What action step is required of me to make this affirmation a maximized reality?

_____
_____
_____
_____
_____
_____
_____

211. I am a survivor of what was done to me in childhood.

GENIUS THOUGHT: Why am I a survivor of my childhood?

_____
_____
_____
_____
_____
_____
_____

GENIUS ACTION: What action step is required of me to make this affirmation a maximized reality?

_____
_____
_____
_____
_____
_____
_____
_____

212. I am ready for the adventure of life.

GENIUS THOUGHT: How am I preparing for the adventure of life?

GENIUS ACTION: What action step is required of me to make this affirmation a maximized reality?

213. I am free of all emotional and financial debt.

GENIUS THOUGHT: Why am I free of all debt?

_____
_____
_____
_____
_____
_____
_____

GENIUS ACTION: What action step is required of me to make this affirmation a maximized reality?

_____
_____
_____
_____
_____
_____
_____

214. I am the king I was born to be.

GENIUS THOUGHT: Why am I a king?

_____
_____
_____
_____
_____
_____
_____

GENIUS ACTION: What action step is required of me to make this affirmation a maximized reality?

_____
_____
_____
_____
_____
_____
_____

215. There is a scholar residing within me whom I welcome to surface.

GENIUS THOUGHT: Why am I a scholar?

_____
_____
_____
_____
_____
_____
_____

GENIUS ACTION: What action step is required of me to make this affirmation a maximized reality?

_____
_____
_____
_____
_____
_____
_____

216. Those who possess light fill my environment.

GENIUS THOUGHT: How is my environment filled by those with light?

_____
_____
_____
_____
_____
_____
_____

GENIUS ACTION: What action step is required of me to make this affirmation a maximized reality?

_____
_____
_____
_____
_____
_____
_____

217. I am an architect of opportunity.

GENIUS THOUGHT: Why am I an architect of opportunity?

_____
_____
_____
_____
_____
_____
_____

GENIUS ACTION: What action step is required of me to make this affirmation a maximized reality?

_____
_____
_____
_____
_____
_____
_____

218. I have more than enough and all of my cups are running over.

GENIUS THOUGHT: Why do I have more than enough?

_____
_____
_____
_____
_____
_____
_____

GENIUS ACTION: What action step is required of me to make this affirmation a maximized reality?

_____
_____
_____
_____
_____
_____
_____

219. The walls of my heart sing songs.

GENIUS THOUGHT: Why do my heart walls sing songs?

GENIUS ACTION: What action step is required of me to make this affirmation a maximized reality?

220. I am committed to grow in grace.

GENIUS THOUGHT: Why am I committed to grow in grace?

_____
_____
_____
_____
_____
_____
_____

GENIUS ACTION: What action step is required of me to make this affirmation a maximized reality?

_____
_____
_____
_____
_____
_____
_____

221. I am good enough.

GENIUS THOUGHT: Why am I good enough?

_____
_____
_____
_____
_____
_____
_____

GENIUS ACTION: What action step is required of me to make this affirmation a maximized reality?

_____
_____
_____
_____
_____
_____
_____

222. I am capable because I am based on a divine blueprint.

GENIUS THOUGHT: How am I capable?

_____
_____
_____
_____
_____
_____
_____

GENIUS ACTION: What action step is required of me to make this affirmation a maximized reality?

_____
_____
_____
_____
_____
_____
_____

223. I embrace every individual I encounter as a soul mate.

GENIUS THOUGHT: Why do I embrace everyone as a soul mate?

_____
_____
_____
_____
_____
_____
_____

GENIUS ACTION: What action step is required of me to make this affirmation a maximized reality?

_____
_____
_____
_____
_____
_____
_____

224. Virtue is in my DNA.

GENIUS THOUGHT: How is virtue in my DNA?

_____
_____
_____
_____
_____
_____
_____

GENIUS ACTION: What action step is required of me to make this affirmation a maximized reality?

_____
_____
_____
_____
_____
_____
_____

225. I am living a new way of thinking.

GENIUS THOUGHT: How am I living a new way of thinking?

_____
_____
_____
_____
_____
_____
_____

GENIUS ACTION: What action step is required of me to make this affirmation a maximized reality?

_____
_____
_____
_____
_____
_____
_____

226. My ambition is what allows me to engage in eternal wealth.

GENIUS THOUGHT: Why do I engage in eternal wealth?

_____
_____
_____
_____
_____
_____
_____

GENIUS ACTION: What action step is required of me to make this affirmation a maximized reality?

_____
_____
_____
_____
_____
_____
_____

227. I am a being who wishes the best of my communal experience.

GENIUS THOUGHT: Why do I wish the best of my communal experience?

GENIUS ACTION: What action step is required of me to make this affirmation a maximized reality?

228. I am not a consumer; I am a producer of light.

GENIUS THOUGHT: How am I a producer of light?

_____
_____
_____
_____
_____
_____
_____

GENIUS ACTION: What action step is required of me to make this affirmation a maximized reality?

_____
_____
_____
_____
_____
_____
_____

229. I am empathetic to the human journey of others.

GENIUS THOUGHT: Why am I empathetic to others?

GENIUS ACTION: What action step is required of me to make this affirmation a maximized reality?

230. At my core I am more than an animal.

GENIUS THOUGHT: How am I more than an animal?

___

GENIUS ACTION: What action step is required of me to make this affirmation a maximized reality?

___

231. The source of my evolution is love intertwined with the energy of peace.

GENIUS THOUGHT: Why is the source of my evolution love, energy and peace?

___

GENIUS ACTION: What action step is required of me to make this affirmation a maximized reality?

232. I am because I belong.

GENIUS THOUGHT: Why do I belong?

_____
_____
_____
_____
_____
_____

GENIUS ACTION: What action step is required of me to make this affirmation a maximized reality?

_____
_____
_____
_____
_____
_____

233. I make and retain friends with ease.

GENIUS THOUGHT: How do I retain friends easily?

_____
_____
_____
_____
_____
_____
_____

GENIUS ACTION: What action step is required of me to make this affirmation a maximized reality?

_____
_____
_____
_____
_____
_____
_____

234. I am the first hero in my child's life.

GENIUS THOUGHT: Why am I the first hero in my child's life?

_____
_____
_____
_____
_____
_____
_____

GENIUS ACTION: What action step is required of me to make this affirmation a maximized reality?

_____
_____
_____
_____
_____
_____
_____

235. I love others, as I love myself.

GENIUS THOUGHT: Why do I love others as myself?

GENIUS ACTION: What action step is required of me to make this affirmation a maximized reality?

236. I allow compassion to enter every aspect of my life.

GENIUS THOUGHT: Why does compassion enter my life?

_____
_____
_____
_____
_____
_____
_____

GENIUS ACTION: What action step is required of me to make this affirmation a maximized reality?

_____
_____
_____
_____
_____
_____
_____

237. My heart is the center of all things.

GENIUS THOUGHT: Why is my heart the center of all things?

_____
_____
_____
_____
_____
_____
_____

GENIUS ACTION: What action step is required of me to make this affirmation a maximized reality?

_____
_____
_____
_____
_____
_____
_____

238. I am connected to all things at all times.

GENIUS THOUGHT: Why am I connected to all things?

___

GENIUS ACTION: What action step is required of me to make this affirmation a maximized reality?

___

239. I am built for this moment in my life.

GENIUS THOUGHT: How am I built for this moment?

_____
_____
_____
_____
_____
_____
_____

GENIUS ACTION: What action step is required of me to make this affirmation a maximized reality?

_____
_____
_____
_____
_____
_____
_____

240. My life is better due to my acceptance of my power.

GENIUS THOUGHT: How have I accepted my power?

GENIUS ACTION: What action step is required of me to make this affirmation a maximized reality?

241. All things work together for my good.

GENIUS THOUGHT: Why do all things work together for my good?

_____
_____
_____
_____
_____
_____
_____

GENIUS ACTION: What action step is required of me to make this affirmation a maximized reality?

_____
_____
_____
_____
_____
_____
_____

242. I share the same breath as the greatest of all living beings; therefore, I AM GREAT.

GENIUS THOUGHT: Why am I great?

_____
_____
_____
_____
_____
_____
_____

GENIUS ACTION: What action step is required of me to make this affirmation a maximized reality?

_____
_____
_____
_____
_____
_____
_____

243. I am kin to all life on Earth.

GENIUS THOUGHT: Why am I kin to all life on Earth?

GENIUS ACTION: What action step is required of me to make this affirmation a maximized reality?

244. I am affected by the needs of my brothers and sisters.

GENIUS THOUGHT: Why am I affected by the needs of my brothers and sisters?

_____
_____
_____
_____
_____
_____
_____

GENIUS ACTION: What action step is required of me to make this affirmation a maximized reality?

_____
_____
_____
_____
_____
_____
_____

245. I am far grander than what I once conceived possible.

GENIUS THOUGHT: Why am I grander that what I once conceived possible?

_____
_____
_____
_____
_____
_____
_____

GENIUS ACTION: What action step is required of me to make this affirmation a maximized reality?

_____
_____
_____
_____
_____
_____
_____

246. I am dedicated to showing men that they matter.

GENIUS THOUGHT: Why am I dedicated to showing men they matter?

_____
_____
_____
_____
_____
_____
_____

GENIUS ACTION: What action step is required of me to make this affirmation a maximized reality?

_____
_____
_____
_____
_____
_____
_____

247. I adhere to cooperation rather than competition.

GENIUS THOUGHT: How do I adhere to cooperation?

___

GENIUS ACTION: What action step is required of me to make this affirmation a maximized reality?

___

248. I shall overcome.

GENIUS THOUGHT: Why shall I overcome?

GENIUS ACTION: What action step is required of me to make this affirmation a maximized reality?

249. I am the beloved of a power greater than myself.

GENIUS THOUGHT: Why am I beloved by a power greater than myself?

_____
_____
_____
_____
_____
_____
_____

GENIUS ACTION: What action step is required of me to make this affirmation a maximized reality?

_____
_____
_____
_____
_____
_____
_____

250. I am creating my personal definition of success.

GENIUS THOUGHT: Why am I creating my personal definition of success?

___

GENIUS ACTION: What action step is required of me to make this affirmation a maximized reality?

___

251. I see God in everyone and everything.

GENIUS THOUGHT: Why do I see God in everyone?

_____
_____
_____
_____
_____
_____

GENIUS ACTION: What action step is required of me to make this affirmation a maximized reality?

_____
_____
_____
_____
_____
_____

252. I delight myself in the field of possibilities.

GENIUS THOUGHT: Why do I have a field of possibilities?

_____
_____
_____
_____
_____
_____
_____

GENIUS ACTION: What action step is required of me to make this affirmation a maximized reality?

_____
_____
_____
_____
_____
_____
_____

253. I am more than what I have accumulated.

GENIUS THOUGHT: Why am I more than I have accumulated?

_____
_____
_____
_____
_____
_____
_____

GENIUS ACTION: What action step is required of me to make this affirmation a maximized reality?

_____
_____
_____
_____
_____
_____
_____

254. I will refrain from raising a good child, because I already have one.

GENIUS THOUGHT: How do I have a good child?

_____
_____
_____
_____
_____
_____
_____

GENIUS ACTION: What action step is required of me to make this affirmation a maximized reality?

_____
_____
_____
_____
_____
_____
_____

255. My feet step in the morning dew of peace.

GENIUS THOUGHT: Why do my feet step in peace?

GENIUS ACTION: What action step is required of me to make this affirmation a maximized reality?

256. I am the hope of chains broken free.

GENIUS THOUGHT: How am I the hope of chains broken free?

_____
_____
_____
_____
_____
_____
_____

GENIUS ACTION: What action step is required of me to make this affirmation a maximized reality?

_____
_____
_____
_____
_____
_____
_____

257. The answer to my mystery is that I am not lost.

GENIUS THOUGHT: Why am I not lost?

_____
_____
_____
_____
_____
_____
_____

GENIUS ACTION: What action step is required of me to make this affirmation a maximized reality?

_____
_____
_____
_____
_____
_____
_____

258. I find value in my response of silence.

GENIUS THOUGHT: Why is there value in my silence?

GENIUS ACTION: What action step is required of me to make this affirmation a maximized reality?

259. As I operate in the present, it frees me of a longing for the future and an unhealthy association with the past.

GENIUS THOUGHT: How does operating in the present affect my future and past?

GENIUS ACTION: What action step is required of me to make this affirmation a maximized reality?

260. I am a gardener of pleasantries.

GENIUS THOUGHT: Why am I a gardener of pleasantries?

GENIUS ACTION: What action step is required of me to make this affirmation a maximized reality?

261. I am creating a dynasty of brave, kind and laughing kings and queens.

GENIUS THOUGHT: Why am I creating a dynasty of kings and queens?

_____
_____
_____
_____
_____
_____
_____

GENIUS ACTION: What action step is required of me to make this affirmation a maximized reality?

_____
_____
_____
_____
_____
_____
_____

262. I am an embodiment of stability and sensitivities.

GENIUS THOUGHT: How do I embody stability and sensitivity?

_____
_____
_____
_____
_____
_____
_____

GENIUS ACTION: What action step is required of me to make this affirmation a maximized reality?

_____
_____
_____
_____
_____
_____
_____

263. Today I shall drink the zest of life like sweet tea on a hillside.

GENIUS THOUGHT: Why do I drink the zest of life?

_____
_____
_____
_____
_____
_____
_____

GENIUS ACTION: What action step is required of me to make this affirmation a maximized reality?

_____
_____
_____
_____
_____
_____
_____

264. I promote a high degree of shamelessness.

GENIUS THOUGHT: Why am I shameless?

GENIUS ACTION: What action step is required of me to make this affirmation a maximized reality?

265. I am wholehearted and sexy.

GENIUS THOUGHT: Why am I so sexy?

_____
_____
_____
_____
_____
_____
_____

GENIUS ACTION: What action step is required of me to make this affirmation a maximized reality?

_____
_____
_____
_____
_____
_____
_____

266. I think I should be who I am.

GENIUS THOUGHT: Why should I be who I am?

___

GENIUS ACTION: What action step is required of me to make this affirmation a maximized reality?

___

267. I am complete within my vulnerability.

GENIUS THOUGHT: Why does my vulnerability allow me to be complete?

_____
_____
_____
_____
_____
_____
_____

GENIUS ACTION: What action step is required of me to make this affirmation a maximized reality?

_____
_____
_____
_____
_____
_____
_____

268. I pledge allegiance to my happiness.

GENIUS THOUGHT: Why do I pledge allegiance to my happiness?

GENIUS ACTION: What action step is required of me to make this affirmation a maximized reality?

269. My children are worthy of my love and influence.

GENIUS THOUGHT: Why are my children worthy of my love?

_____
_____
_____
_____
_____
_____
_____

GENIUS ACTION: What action step is required of me to make this affirmation a maximized reality?

_____
_____
_____
_____
_____
_____
_____

270. I am the greatest.

GENIUS THOUGHT: Why am I the greatest?

___

GENIUS ACTION: What action step is required of me to make this affirmation a maximized reality?

___

271. My body is built for passion.

GENIUS THOUGHT: How is my body built for passion?

_____
_____
_____
_____
_____
_____
_____

GENIUS ACTION: What action step is required of me to make this affirmation a maximized reality?

_____
_____
_____
_____
_____
_____
_____

272. I matter.

GENIUS THOUGHT: Why do I matter?

GENIUS ACTION: What action step is required of me to make this affirmation a maximized reality?

273. I have daily installments of euphoria.

GENIUS THOUGHT: Why do I have installments of euphoria?

GENIUS ACTION: What action step is required of me to make this affirmation a maximized reality?

274. I have an expectation that today will be a gift of jubilation.

GENIUS THOUGHT: How will today be a gift of jubilation?

_____
_____
_____
_____
_____
_____
_____

GENIUS ACTION: What action step is required of me to make this affirmation a maximized reality?

_____
_____
_____
_____
_____
_____
_____

275. I inhale support and exhale charity.

GENIUS THOUGHT: Why do I breathe support and charity?

GENIUS ACTION: What action step is required of me to make this affirmation a maximized reality?

276. I take refuge in the heart chamber of God.

GENIUS THOUGHT: Why can I take refuge in the heart of God?

_____
_____
_____
_____
_____
_____
_____

GENIUS ACTION: What action step is required of me to make this affirmation a maximized reality?

_____
_____
_____
_____
_____
_____
_____

277. I am blessed.

GENIUS THOUGHT: Why am I blessed?

GENIUS ACTION: What action step is required of me to make this affirmation a maximized reality?

278. Favor envelopes me.

GENIUS THOUGHT: How does favor envelope me?

_____
_____
_____
_____
_____
_____
_____

GENIUS ACTION: What action step is required of me to make this affirmation a maximized reality?

_____
_____
_____
_____
_____
_____
_____

279. I feast upon dreams and blessings.

GENIUS THOUGHT: Why do I feast upon dreams and blessings?

GENIUS ACTION: What action step is required of me to make this affirmation a maximized reality?

280. From this moment I will glorify the best I have inside myself.

GENIUS THOUGHT: How will I glorify the best in myself?

_____
_____
_____
_____
_____
_____
_____

GENIUS ACTION: What action step is required of me to make this affirmation a maximized reality?

_____
_____
_____
_____
_____
_____
_____

281. I offer love that holds people where they are and embraces their imperfections.

GENIUS THOUGHT: Why do I offer love?

_____
_____
_____
_____
_____
_____
_____

GENIUS ACTION: What action step is required of me to make this affirmation a maximized reality?

_____
_____
_____
_____
_____
_____
_____

282. My hope will make all the difference.

GENIUS THOUGHT: Why does my hope make all the difference?

_____
_____
_____
_____
_____
_____
_____

GENIUS ACTION: What action step is required of me to make this affirmation a maximized reality?

_____
_____
_____
_____
_____
_____
_____

283. As a man, I am the unveiling of nirvana.

GENIUS THOUGHT: How am I the unveiling of nirvana?

_____
_____
_____
_____
_____
_____
_____

GENIUS ACTION: What action step is required of me to make this affirmation a maximized reality?

_____
_____
_____
_____
_____
_____
_____

284. I am anointed for victory.

GENIUS THOUGHT: Why am I anointed for victory?

GENIUS ACTION: What action step is required of me to make this affirmation a maximized reality?

285. All things are lessons and I am willing to learn.

GENIUS THOUGHT: Why are all things lessons?

GENIUS ACTION: What action step is required of me to make this affirmation a maximized reality?

286. My hurts and my pains are valid.

GENIUS THOUGHT: Why are my hurts valid?

___

GENIUS ACTION: What action step is required of me to make this affirmation a maximized reality?

___

287. I take pride in the process of my progression.

GENIUS THOUGHT: How do I take pride in my progression?

___
___
___
___
___
___
___

GENIUS ACTION: What action step is required of me to make this affirmation a maximized reality?

___
___
___
___
___
___
___

288. I believe in the magnificence of me.

GENIUS THOUGHT: Why do I believe in my magnificence?

_____
_____
_____
_____
_____
_____
_____

GENIUS ACTION: What action step is required of me to make this affirmation a maximized reality?

_____
_____
_____
_____
_____
_____
_____

289. My predictions are bathed in success.

GENIUS THOUGHT: Why are my predictions bathed in success?

_____
_____
_____
_____
_____
_____
_____

GENIUS ACTION: What action step is required of me to make this affirmation a maximized reality?

_____
_____
_____
_____
_____
_____
_____

290. I am worth following.

GENIUS THOUGHT: Why am I worth following?

_____
_____
_____
_____
_____
_____

GENIUS ACTION: What action step is required of me to make this affirmation a maximized reality?

_____
_____
_____
_____
_____
_____

291. I am timeless in my ability to be of service.

GENIUS THOUGHT: How am I timeless in my ability to be of service?

_____
_____
_____
_____
_____
_____
_____

GENIUS ACTION: What action step is required of me to make this affirmation a maximized reality?

_____
_____
_____
_____
_____
_____
_____

292. I am the walking, breathing, feeling definition of what a man is.

GENIUS THOUGHT: Why am I the definition of what a man is?

_____
_____
_____
_____
_____
_____
_____

GENIUS ACTION: What action step is required of me to make this affirmation a maximized reality?

_____
_____
_____
_____
_____
_____
_____

293. I am exactly where I need to be.

GENIUS THOUGHT: Why am I exactly where I need to be?

_____
_____
_____
_____
_____
_____

GENIUS ACTION: What action step is required of me to make this affirmation a maximized reality?

_____
_____
_____
_____
_____
_____

294. I once lived from crisis to crisis: I now live from blessing to blessing.

GENIUS THOUGHT: How do I live from blessing to blessing?

_____
_____
_____
_____
_____
_____
_____

GENIUS ACTION: What action step is required of me to make this affirmation a maximized reality?

_____
_____
_____
_____
_____
_____
_____

295. I am in love with my life.

GENIUS THOUGHT: Why am I in love with my life?

_____
_____
_____
_____
_____
_____
_____

GENIUS ACTION: What action step is required of me to make this affirmation a maximized reality?

_____
_____
_____
_____
_____
_____
_____

296. My happiness is a priority.

GENIUS THOUGHT: Why is my happiness a priority?

GENIUS ACTION: What action step is required of me to make this affirmation a maximized reality?

297. I am fulfilled with who I am right now.

GENIUS THOUGHT: Why am I fulfilled with who I am?

_____
_____
_____
_____
_____
_____
_____

GENIUS ACTION: What action step is required of me to make this affirmation a maximized reality?

_____
_____
_____
_____
_____
_____
_____

298. I am able to age remarkably and without fear.

GENIUS THOUGHT: How am I able to age without fear?

_____
_____
_____
_____
_____
_____
_____

GENIUS ACTION: What action step is required of me to make this affirmation a maximized reality?

_____
_____
_____
_____
_____
_____
_____

299. My vision is attainable.

GENIUS THOUGHT: Why is my vision attainable?

_____
_____
_____
_____
_____
_____
_____

GENIUS ACTION: What action step is required of me to make this affirmation a maximized reality?

_____
_____
_____
_____
_____
_____
_____

300. I was not a mistake; I am an ingenious surprise.

GENIUS THOUGHT: Why am I an ingenious surprise?

_____
_____
_____
_____
_____
_____
_____

GENIUS ACTION: What action step is required of me to make this affirmation a maximized reality?

_____
_____
_____
_____
_____
_____
_____

301. I am more than a repairman; I am a dreamer.

GENIUS THOUGHT: Why am I a dreamer?

___

GENIUS ACTION: What action step is required of me to make this affirmation a maximized reality?

___

302. I am the totality of my purpose rather than my possessions.

GENIUS THOUGHT: How am I the totality of my purpose?

___

GENIUS ACTION: What action step is required of me to make this affirmation a maximized reality?

___

303. I am worth showing up for.

GENIUS THOUGHT: Why am I worth showing up for?

_____
_____
_____
_____
_____
_____
_____

GENIUS ACTION: What action step is required of me to make this affirmation a maximized reality?

_____
_____
_____
_____
_____
_____
_____

304. What anyone thinks about me is none of my business.

GENIUS THOUGHT: Why is it none of my business what people think about me?

_____
_____
_____
_____
_____
_____
_____

GENIUS ACTION: What action step is required of me to make this affirmation a maximized reality?

_____
_____
_____
_____
_____
_____
_____

305. I am proud of my ability to hustle.

GENIUS THOUGHT: Why am I proud of my ability to hustle?

_____
_____
_____
_____
_____
_____
_____

GENIUS ACTION: What action step is required of me to make this affirmation a maximized reality?

_____
_____
_____
_____
_____
_____
_____

306. My mind is vast and mesmerizing.

GENIUS THOUGHT: How is my mind vast?

_____
_____
_____
_____
_____
_____

GENIUS ACTION: What action step is required of me to make this affirmation a maximized reality?

_____
_____
_____
_____
_____
_____

307. I attract the good in people and situations.

GENIUS THOUGHT: How do I attract the good in people?

_____
_____
_____
_____
_____
_____
_____

GENIUS ACTION: What action step is required of me to make this affirmation a maximized reality?

_____
_____
_____
_____
_____
_____
_____

308. I am adored.

GENIUS THOUGHT: Why am I adored?

GENIUS ACTION: What action step is required of me to make this affirmation a maximized reality?

309. I believe that I am important.

GENIUS THOUGHT: Why am I important?

_____
_____
_____
_____
_____
_____
_____

GENIUS ACTION: What action step is required of me to make this affirmation a maximized reality?

_____
_____
_____
_____
_____
_____
_____

310. My behavior allows me to enjoy wealth in every aspect of my life without guilt.

GENIUS THOUGHT: Why do I enjoy wealth without guilt?

_____
_____
_____
_____
_____
_____
_____

GENIUS ACTION: What action step is required of me to make this affirmation a maximized reality?

_____
_____
_____
_____
_____
_____
_____

311. I am the personification of hundreds of years of perseverance.

GENIUS THOUGHT: How am I the personification of perseverance?

_____
_____
_____
_____
_____
_____
_____

GENIUS ACTION: What action step is required of me to make this affirmation a maximized reality?

_____
_____
_____
_____
_____
_____
_____

312. I am the master of time. It serves me well.

GENIUS THOUGHT: Why does time serve me well?

GENIUS ACTION: What action step is required of me to make this affirmation a maximized reality?

313. I excel and profit from change at every level.

GENIUS THOUGHT: How do I profit from change?

GENIUS ACTION: What action step is required of me to make this affirmation a maximized reality?

314. I am gifted, supreme and privileged beyond comprehension.

GENIUS THOUGHT: Why am I gifted beyond comprehension?

_____
_____
_____
_____
_____
_____
_____

GENIUS ACTION: What action step is required of me to make this affirmation a maximized reality?

_____
_____
_____
_____
_____
_____
_____

315. I am a life altering treasure.

GENIUS THOUGHT: Why am I a life altering treasure?

_____
_____
_____
_____
_____
_____
_____

GENIUS ACTION: What action step is required of me to make this affirmation a maximized reality?

_____
_____
_____
_____
_____
_____
_____

316. I am renewed by the sensation of bliss.

GENIUS THOUGHT: Why do I have a sensation of bliss?

GENIUS ACTION: What action step is required of me to make this affirmation a maximized reality?

317. I am thankful for the transformation of knowing better.

GENIUS THOUGHT: How do I know better?

_____
_____
_____
_____
_____
_____
_____

GENIUS ACTION: What action step is required of me to make this affirmation a maximized reality?

_____
_____
_____
_____
_____
_____
_____

318. I am delighted to find myself complete.

GENIUS THOUGHT: How am I complete?

GENIUS ACTION: What action step is required of me to make this affirmation a maximized reality?

319. I must keep going because my journey is more important than fear.

GENIUS THOUGHT: Why is my journey more important than fear?

GENIUS ACTION: What action step is required of me to make this affirmation a maximized reality?

320. I choose to be understanding rather than right.

GENIUS THOUGHT: Why is it important to be understanding rather than right?

_____
_____
_____
_____
_____
_____
_____

GENIUS ACTION: What action step is required of me to make this affirmation a maximized reality?

_____
_____
_____
_____
_____
_____
_____

321. I reign from a throne of love rather than fear.

GENIUS THOUGHT: Why do I reign from a throne of love?

_____
_____
_____
_____
_____
_____
_____

GENIUS ACTION: What action step is required of me to make this affirmation a maximized reality?

_____
_____
_____
_____
_____
_____
_____

322. I am poised for a breakthrough.

GENIUS THOUGHT: Why am I poised for a breakthrough?

_____
_____
_____
_____
_____
_____
_____

GENIUS ACTION: What action step is required of me to make this affirmation a maximized reality?

_____
_____
_____
_____
_____
_____
_____

323. I am expecting waves of inspiration.

GENIUS THOUGHT: Why am I expecting waves of inspiration?

_____
_____
_____
_____
_____
_____
_____

GENIUS ACTION: What action step is required of me to make this affirmation a maximized reality?

_____
_____
_____
_____
_____
_____
_____

324. I am removed from delighting in dysfunction; I now delight in dreams.

GENIUS THOUGHT: Why do I delight in dreams?

GENIUS ACTION: What action step is required of me to make this affirmation a maximized reality?

325. I am a proclamation of treasure.

GENIUS THOUGHT: How am I a proclamation of treasure?

GENIUS ACTION: What action step is required of me to make this affirmation a maximized reality?

326. I am fulfilled by the absence of envy.

GENIUS THOUGHT: Why am I absent of envy?

_____
_____
_____
_____
_____
_____
_____

GENIUS ACTION: What action step is required of me to make this affirmation a maximized reality?

_____
_____
_____
_____
_____
_____
_____

327. My identity is enhanced through meditation.

GENIUS THOUGHT: Why does meditation enhance my identity?

_____
_____
_____
_____
_____
_____

GENIUS ACTION: What action step is required of me to make this affirmation a maximized reality?

_____
_____
_____
_____
_____
_____

328. I am the stillness of the horizon.

GENIUS THOUGHT: Why am I the stillness of the horizon?

GENIUS ACTION: What action step is required of me to make this affirmation a maximized reality?

329. The worst is over.

GENIUS THOUGHT: Why is the worst over?

_____
_____
_____
_____
_____
_____
_____

GENIUS ACTION: What action step is required of me to make this affirmation a maximized reality?

_____
_____
_____
_____
_____
_____
_____

330. The bliss I breathe is invigorating.

GENIUS THOUGHT: Why is my bliss invigorating?

GENIUS ACTION: What action step is required of me to make this affirmation a maximized reality?

331. I face challenges head on without excuses.

GENIUS THOUGHT: How do I face challenges without excuses?

GENIUS ACTION: What action step is required of me to make this affirmation a maximized reality?

332. I conceive achievement effortlessly.

GENIUS THOUGHT: Why do I conceive effortless achievement?

GENIUS ACTION: What action step is required of me to make this affirmation a maximized reality?

333. My smile is medicinal.

GENIUS THOUGHT: How is my smile medicinal?

_____
_____
_____
_____
_____
_____
_____

GENIUS ACTION: What action step is required of me to make this affirmation a maximized reality?

_____
_____
_____
_____
_____
_____
_____

334. My dream is chasing me.

GENIUS THOUGHT: Why is my dream chasing me?

_____
_____
_____
_____
_____
_____
_____

GENIUS ACTION: What action step is required of me to make this affirmation a maximized reality?

_____
_____
_____
_____
_____
_____
_____

335. I was born ready.

GENIUS THOUGHT: How was I born ready?

GENIUS ACTION: What action step is required of me to make this affirmation a maximized reality?

336. My hustle muscle is strong.

GENIUS THOUGHT: Why is my hustle muscle so strong?

_____
_____
_____
_____
_____
_____
_____

GENIUS ACTION: What action step is required of me to make this affirmation a maximized reality?

_____
_____
_____
_____
_____
_____
_____

337. Today I danced because I tasted my future.

GENIUS THOUGHT: How did I taste my future?

_____
_____
_____
_____
_____
_____
_____

GENIUS ACTION: What action step is required of me to make this affirmation a maximized reality?

_____
_____
_____
_____
_____
_____
_____

338. I build empires for fun.

GENIUS THOUGHT: Why is it fun to build empires?

_____
_____
_____
_____
_____
_____
_____

GENIUS ACTION: What action step is required of me to make this affirmation a maximized reality?

_____
_____
_____
_____
_____
_____
_____

339. I am shedding all that is untrue about me.

GENIUS THOUGHT: Why am I shedding all that is untrue?

GENIUS ACTION: What action step is required of me to make this affirmation a maximized reality?

340. I will celebrate others from my abundant self-esteem.

GENIUS THOUGHT: Why do I abundantly celebrate others?

GENIUS ACTION: What action step is required of me to make this affirmation a maximized reality?

341. I am highly blissaplined.

GENIUS THOUGHT: Why am I highly blissaplined?

_____
_____
_____
_____
_____
_____
_____

GENIUS ACTION: What action step is required of me to make this affirmation a maximized reality?

_____
_____
_____
_____
_____
_____
_____

342. Folks are delighted by my groove.

GENIUS THOUGHT: Why are folks delighted by my groove?

_____
_____
_____
_____
_____
_____
_____

GENIUS ACTION: What action step is required of me to make this affirmation a maximized reality?

_____
_____
_____
_____
_____
_____
_____

343. I take pleasure in how good my day will be.

GENIUS THOUGHT: Why will I take pleasure in how good my day will be?

_____
_____
_____
_____
_____
_____
_____

GENIUS ACTION: What action step is required of me to make this affirmation a maximized reality?

_____
_____
_____
_____
_____
_____
_____

344. My life will have a happy ending.

GENIUS THOUGHT: How will my life have a happy ending?

_____
_____
_____
_____
_____
_____
_____

GENIUS ACTION: What action step is required of me to make this affirmation a maximized reality?

_____
_____
_____
_____
_____
_____
_____

345. I have created a life where a vacation is not needed.

GENIUS THOUGHT: Why does my life not need a vacation?

_____
_____
_____
_____
_____
_____
_____

GENIUS ACTION: What action step is required of me to make this affirmation a maximized reality?

_____
_____
_____
_____
_____
_____
_____

346. I am open to be held.

GENIUS THOUGHT: Why am I open to being held?

_____
_____
_____
_____
_____
_____
_____

GENIUS ACTION: What action step is required of me to make this affirmation a maximized reality?

_____
_____
_____
_____
_____
_____
_____

347. I am the best man that I can be.

GENIUS THOUGHT: How am I the best man I can be?

_____
_____
_____
_____
_____
_____
_____

GENIUS ACTION: What action step is required of me to make this affirmation a maximized reality?

_____
_____
_____
_____
_____
_____
_____

348. I now choose to live in emotional honesty; I am now honest about what and how I feel.

GENIUS THOUGHT: How am I honest about what and how I feel?

_____
_____
_____
_____
_____
_____
_____

GENIUS ACTION: What action step is required of me to make this affirmation a maximized reality?

_____
_____
_____
_____
_____
_____
_____

349. I have learned to close my eyes at times to see what is important.

GENIUS THOUGHT: What important do I see when I close my eyes?

_____
_____
_____
_____
_____
_____
_____

GENIUS ACTION: What action step is required of me to make this affirmation a maximized reality?

_____
_____
_____
_____
_____
_____
_____

350. I honor the lives of my children.

GENIUS THOUGHT: Why do I honor the lives of my children?

_____
_____
_____
_____
_____
_____
_____

GENIUS ACTION: What action step is required of me to make this affirmation a maximized reality?

_____
_____
_____
_____
_____
_____
_____

351. I am boundless.

GENIUS THOUGHT: Why am I boundless?

_____
_____
_____
_____
_____
_____

GENIUS ACTION: What action step is required of me to make this affirmation a maximized reality?

_____
_____
_____
_____
_____
_____

352. I praise my life partner as a depiction of divine duality.

GENIUS THOUGHT: How is my life partner a depiction of divine duality?

_____
_____
_____
_____
_____
_____
_____

GENIUS ACTION: What action step is required of me to make this affirmation a maximized reality?

_____
_____
_____
_____
_____
_____
_____

353. Purpose and promotions are the bricks that I use to build my mansion.

GENIUS THOUGHT: Why do I build my mansion with purpose and promotions?

GENIUS ACTION: What action step is required of me to make this affirmation a maximized reality?

---

354. I am a human thermostat; instead of becoming a byproduct of my surroundings I change my environment to what suits me best.

GENIUS THOUGHT: How do I change my environment?

_____
_____
_____
_____
_____
_____
_____

GENIUS ACTION: What action step is required of me to make this affirmation a maximized reality?

_____
_____
_____
_____
_____
_____
_____

355. I am safe and secure from all harm.

GENIUS THOUGHT: How am I safe and secure?

_____
_____
_____
_____
_____
_____

GENIUS ACTION: What action step is required of me to make this affirmation a maximized reality?

_____
_____
_____
_____
_____
_____
_____

356. I am visible and recognizable.

GENIUS THOUGHT: Why am I visible and recognizable?

GENIUS ACTION: What action step is required of me to make this affirmation a maximized reality?

357. I am in control of the words and terms that define me.

GENIUS THOUGHT: Why am I in control of what defines me?

_____
_____
_____
_____
_____
_____
_____

GENIUS ACTION: What action step is required of me to make this affirmation a maximized reality?

_____
_____
_____
_____
_____
_____
_____

358. I am the ONLY point of reference for perfection.

GENIUS THOUGHT: Why am I the only point of reference for perfection?

_____
_____
_____
_____
_____
_____

GENIUS ACTION: What action step is required of me to make this affirmation a maximized reality?

_____
_____
_____
_____
_____
_____

359. I am the conductor of the symphony called "My Life."

GENIUS THOUGHT: Why am I the conductor of my life?

___

GENIUS ACTION: What action step is required of me to make this affirmation a maximized reality?

___

360. My dreams are delightfully doable.

GENIUS THOUGHT: How are my dreams doable?

_____
_____
_____
_____
_____
_____

GENIUS ACTION: What action step is required of me to make this affirmation a maximized reality?

_____
_____
_____
_____
_____
_____

361. I forgive myself today for yesterday.

GENIUS THOUGHT: Why do I forgive myself for yesterday?

_____
_____
_____
_____
_____
_____
_____

GENIUS ACTION: What action step is required of me to make this affirmation a maximized reality?

_____
_____
_____
_____
_____
_____
_____

362. I am one with all that is.

GENIUS THOUGHT: How am I one with all that is?

_____
_____
_____
_____
_____
_____

GENIUS ACTION: What action step is required of me to make this affirmation a maximized reality?

_____
_____
_____
_____
_____
_____

363. I am a cosmic incubator of masculine possibility.

GENIUS THOUGHT: How am I an incubator of masculine possibility?

_____
_____
_____
_____
_____
_____

GENIUS ACTION: What action step is required of me to make this affirmation a maximized reality?

_____
_____
_____
_____
_____
_____

364. I am more valuable than a changed tire or working disposal.

GENIUS THOUGHT: Why am I more valuable than a changed tire?

_____
_____
_____
_____
_____
_____
_____

GENIUS ACTION: What action step is required of me to make this affirmation a maximized reality?

_____
_____
_____
_____
_____
_____
_____

365. I am man enough.

GENIUS THOUGHT: Why am I man enough?

GENIUS ACTION: What action step is required of me to make this affirmation a maximized reality?

www.ingramcontent.com/pod-product-compliance
Lightning Source LLC
Chambersburg PA
CBHW072001150426
43194CB00008B/949